Waking the D

Norse Myth, Folklore, Runes and Magic

ANDREAS KORNEVALL

GREEN MAGIC

Green Magic
53 Brooks Road
Street
Somerset
BA16 0PP
England
www.greenmagicpublishing.com

Designed and typeset by Carrigboy, Wells, UK
www.carrigboy.co.uk

ISBN 9781739973384

GREEN MAGIC

Contents

CONTENTS

Acknowledgements

This book would not be possible without the help from the editing eyes and insight of Harry Horner. I also owe a debt of gratitude to all the people at the School of Myth in Devon, and Dr. Martin Shaw, a teacher and friend of the mysteries. For advice and their encouragement I wish to also thank Rev. Peter Owen Jones and David Hodgson.

I also want to thank my family, my daughters Chloe and Rosie, whose imaginations can eclipse a star and whose joy in the spark of life is always infectious. Also, big thanks for ongoing support as always from my family in Sweden – Christian, Pia and Sandra.

Last, but not least, thank you to my great Amor, Vicky, who has been with me every step of the way with unwavering support all through the seasons.

I had a Dream

The bright sun was a Sun-King Serpent and the stars the scales on its back. His vertebrae were the constellations, from his vigour of fire and from his own willpower; the Sun-King Serpent had taken dominion of the known worlds.

All hearts sung self-serving prayers to save only themselves. People lived for their desires, then flames started to burn in all directions, casting the world into an ocean of ash.

Desperate souls gathered around to look and admire the Sun-King Serpent's crown which contained a fearful vision of what will come to pass.

The brows of men and women shone dull and grey by the Sun-King Serpent's light. When doom fell upon them, some tried to fight, but most only wept.

Whilst the cries of famine were heard, the Serpent Sun-King gorged himself in the ashen shadows of the world.

When people died, bones were gathered into dark tombs, unnamed and forgotten.

The rule of the Sun-King Serpent had made the world lifeless, silent and without season. For mankind, there was only desolation, in ruin the world lay.

All obeyed the Sun-King Serpent.

All.

Save one.

Her name was Goldwinde.

The crowd beheld her when she stood defiant, they beheld her when she refused to bend her knee in submission to the power of the Sun-King Serpent.

She was the ancient witch who had burnt thrice on the stake to come back to life from the flames again, the ancient witch who had once made a truce between the gods of the sky and the gods of nature.

The people gazed upon her uncontaminated beauty. She was naked as the waves in the sea. Her only garment was the girdle of emotion, lined with the dream of harvest and birth upon her waist; she was alive with bright sentience. Her eyes were cornflowers and her hair flowed and oscillated in the hot winds of the cold-hearted world.

Palpitating in the ashes, the gathering crowd groped at her with ravenous, hungry and searching hands, to grasp, to hold and to consume.

She began to chant from an age-old verse, from a rediscovered reservoir of thought.

Her song was heard once upon a life, once upon a moment, and once upon a time.

Expectation was roused within the rivers, seas and lakes, all life responded to her melodic incantation; the Moon in her command and magic entered the silent depths of soul.

Darkness was transformed into the mother of light as she weaved the thread of fate.

Pierced by the Sun King Serpent's eyes, she endured, she responded with words of freedom, of chains breaking, of waters cascading and she revealed his violations.

The Sun-King Serpent coiled in his galactic frame.

Bravery wrapped around her, she vanquished the spell of the devoured world, the crown of the Sun-King Serpent fell.

Under a waxed moon's glare, he was only a snake in her hands.

Fear was subdued.

A faint light grew.

Stories, Myths and Meaning

THE ANCIENT GRANDMOTHER

In 1643 an Icelandic bishop called Brynjolf Sveinsson was given forty-five pieces of vellum containing poetry and prose. The words on this vellum are thought to have been written down sometime around 1270. Which person, or family, had protected this manuscript for over 400 years, we do not know, but we can be sure that it would have been a treacherous secret to bear safely through the medieval witch-burning centuries; it had been hidden from public view to protect it from being destroyed by the representatives of the Roman Christian Church.

The bishop did not himself keep the manuscript and neither did he hold it above a flame; instead, he offered the collection as a gift to the King of Denmark. This manuscript came to be known as the Codex Regius as a result. There it remained, in Copenhagen, until 1971 when it was returned to Iceland. Warships had to transport the manuscript across the sea, as a plane journey was seen as too risky; such was the preciousness of the cargo. That is not surprising as these vellum papers represent the few written remains we have of northern European pre-Christian culture. They are known today by the collective name of the Eddas. Many experts, and scholars, debate what the intriguing word "Eddas" means etymologically. My preferred explanation is: "the Ancient Grandmother."

What stories do we find hidden amongst these ancient animal skins?

These are stories that speak of beginnings and endings, of great conflicts, betrayal, murder and self-sacrifice for the greater good. There is a lesson about what happens when we try to harness the power of giants. Supernatural beings found within their pages include gods, goddesses, trolls, dwarves, dragons, elves and many other beasts and monsters that are particular to the landscapes of northern Europe.

Why should we care about tales this old?

Perhaps one of the best definitions of mythology comes from the fourth century writer Sallustius:

"Myths are things which never happened, but always are."

This phrase teaches us a great deal about the mythical imagination: that it does not merely reflect the travails of our human life, but guides us through the longings, yearnings and the existential search for our hidden human soul. When reading these myths, even today, we create worlds of meaning.

MYTHOS AND LOGOS

In ancient Greece, "logos" was the objective language, the non-personal; you presented it in court with facts and figures – the evidence-based language. Logos was the peer-reviewed essay, the analysis, the laboratory, the bookkeeping. Since that time, and as a heritage from ancient Greece and the influence of the enlightenment period, our Western society presents logos as the main, and only, viable description of reality and truth; a reality and truth that can be calculated and quantified.

But is this language enough? Is science enough to explain your feelings when you look into the eyes of the person you love?

The anathema of logos is "mythos". It is subjective, the personal; the oral story, the poetry – mythos speaks of eagles carrying golden keys, and of the Earth being created in seven days; it speaks of gods riding through the rainbow bridge. Mythos doesn't only see the Sun, but an entire golden chariot driven by the Sun Goddess, Sol, riding across the sky. Her horses are on fire as she rises from the gates of the east.

Both mythos and logos are necessary in order to attain philosophical knowledge and wisdom. The laboratory of science and the one of alchemy can live side by side; one using acids and bases, the other the spilled ink of the poet.

The atheist and the Baptist preacher can be in harmony with each other. Because their languages have a different purpose, great insight (and culture) arise from both views.

Fundamentalism arises when mythos tries to infiltrate into the world of logos; suddenly the poetic and mythological language is taken as literal truth and people demand evidence for the eagle that carries the golden key; does it fly through Manchester or Philadelphia?

We want to quantify it and seek evidence for it. Therefore, religious fundamentalism can be seen as a modern phenomenon, trying to explain mythos with logos' terms and conditions. It's a proposition that always ends in vain.

To break this spell, we need to recognize mythos for its own value, insight and wisdom. Seven days in the world of myth means billions of years in the world of science.

We don't need to discredit either science or the fairytale. Mythos is necessary; we need it at funerals, at weddings and when a baby is born. It is a language that shows a reflection of our humanity and it carries metaphorical and poetic depth. We need logos too; in the laboratory, to build a house, in calculating the speed of sound and the mathematics of the revolving galaxy.

Mythos and logos are two continents and we are better off allowing both to co-exist, rather than having an unnecessary tug of war between them, or forcing them together.

This writing is in service to mythos and the deep imagination. The stories told are from the storyteller's chair, born from the hum of rain on the tent canvas and the campfire.

THE WITCH AND THE FUTURE

One day at Birka, Sweden, two missionaries approached an old witch. She was furious when she saw them coming towards her with their bibles, crosses and dark gowns. Witches and missionaries are not the best of friends.

She looked at them and asked:

"Is the god you are bringing omnipresent and all-knowing?"

They responded "Yes" with confidence.

"Can he tell the future?" She asked.

They responded, "Well He can, He is the beginning and the end, He knows all past, present and future, He is the Alpha and the Omega.

She cackled, "This makes your god only a half-god, powerless and he should not come to these lands!" She shouted, spat and turned her back at them.

They crossed themselves at her heretic outburst.

"What do you mean?" They asked.

"Because, if he knows the future, then he has no power to change it." She responded.

The missionaries tried to retort back, "But that is not true, because as He is omniscient, He can also change it."

She looked back at them.

"Then, whatever he was thinking about the future before he changed it, was wrong!"

This dialogue confronts a dilemma that exists between the Christian and Heathen worldviews. If there is a god that knows our fate and destiny, then there is nothing we can do, we are unable to change the course of events. The three sisters of time are called Urd, Verdandi and Skuld. Past, present and future. The word Skuld, depicting the future, means "hidden" – also this is the same root word as "debt" in many Scandinavian languages. If the future is unknown and an open frontier, then we are the ones who can create it. When we practice any form of magic, we are bending our will and power to create something new, to thread a new path, to release from an old wound. This is sometimes called the "art of influencing events." We are not talking about miracles, but about mindful steps that can bring about a more resonant future pathway for ourselves as well as society. We have our fate in our own hands and with this our ethics must respond and that can be a difficult and an expansive freedom to come to terms with.

For example, in the northern European languages we cannot conjugate a verb into a future tense. We can't "mangerais" (future tense of eat), as they say in French. Instead, in the English language we "will" ourselves in order to eat tomorrow – we must add "will" before the verb in order to communicate a future idea. Even though most of us have forgotten the Norn "Skuld", our language is as pagan as the hills because when we "will" something to happen – we are practicing magic.

It stands to reason, if we've engaged passively in a collective forgetting, how do we reverse that process?

Remembering the roots of our language is enough to begin to unlock more of its power.

CHAPTER 1

Time and Memory – Remembering

MYTHOS OF TIME AND THE THREE NORNS

Wherever time is free and eternal, it has no purpose; it counts no stars nor follows any movements. It is when we have decay and death that time reveals itself.

In Norse myth, Memory (personified as Mimir) had a daughter called Urd. Urd is the Goddess of the Cycles of Time, all of time flowed toward her like currents of sea and she received all; she is all of the past. The memory of yesterday transforms into her Urd-water (named Aurr); she collects each wavelet and fills the great Well of Memory. This water in turn grows the eternal tree, Yggdrasil, our Anima Universalis.

This Well of Memory is the source of all ceremonial life. Through ceremony we return to the well and to cyclical time. The water cycle springs upwards through the trunk of Yggdrasil like sap and outwards to the flowering time, which is ever-present. The leaves grow in the present, until the water sinks back into the well carrying all the experiences as it flows into the submerged depths. It flows down to feed the roots, and then the cycle repeats itself again. The eternal tree is vulnerable to our forgetfulness. Forgetfulness causes drought and wildfires and empties the well that feeds the tree. With remembering in ceremony, we grow its leaves. Too much forgetting is an ecological disaster.

This Aurr water can be seen as the original mirror of the world, not the artificial mirror which is there to flatter us, but instead, the water mirror that reflects what is.

The flowers of the tree are tended by Urd's younger sister, Verdandi. Through her, the flowers grow in the ever-present. The movement towards the future is presided over by the third sister, Skuld, her face hidden and cloaked. When the future is hidden, we must awaken our awareness to the choices we make; to be aware of our speech and action. Our morality becomes significant within the confines of a hidden future, just as time is precious when the world is finite and, as we partake in shaping the future, we are accountable for what is happening to the world we inhabit.

At the end of life, we travel towards the past, like flowers falling in the autumn light. Our lives become memories, feeding the deep roots of time in the great well.

All loss is praised from these waters and two swans swim on its mirrored surface, signifying the symbol of Frey – the God of Love.

The Well of Memory is the source and the place where all stories live, from the wreckage of our time it shows us that new flowers are being readied to bud, new paths begin to form.

This water cycle is also an anthropomorphism of the Universe – as above, so below. When Sophia (wisdom) was looking for Bythos (the one), she sought the dark water at the deepest part of the well. Within she entered, and her descent into that darkness precipitated her ascent into wisdom.

The Allfather (Odin) sacrificed his eye into the deep well and it was there that he learnt a hidden knowledge and the runes. His one eye is still there looking into the depths of time, into the waters of the unconscious. The eye sees into the imagination of the world, locating the landscapes of soul, where dreams, memories and fantasies form a spiritual extension, a window, an opening to the inner life of humanity and gods and goddesses.

Note that this mythic thinking is a form of vocabulary of sensations, of our innate and natural understanding of who we are. We learn that there is a watery substance in us that can feed the roots of life through remembrance.

When we have the courage to submerge ourselves and gaze into the deep well within, we emerge with the present flowering of time.

THE UR-LOG: THE ORIGINAL LAWS

The primal laws are called Ur-Log in Old Norse texts (Ur = origin, log = law). These laws relate to the constant unfolding of the cosmos. The consequences of these ancient laws are called the Wyrd.

Where do we find these ancient laws and how can we begin to read them? Within all cultures, the creation myth is that which carries the great story of the cosmos and the narrative of how it all began. To understand each beginning, we need to investigate the creation myth and read its images through the language of mythos to learn about the primal laws.

To visualize the concept better, you can think of it as a stone that has fallen into a lake and caused a circular ripple to form in the water. Once the stone has hit the surface you cannot "undo" the action. All those ripples are the Ur-log (events) in your own life and you are the one throwing the stone – a metaphor here for your actions, thoughts and words.

There can be big stones and small stones. When the ripples from all the stones are combined, it then creates an effect which is called Wyrd – the web of life. Wyrd has an inexhaustible complexity and countless patterns. Every single part of its surface is interlinked and totally dependent on every other part, as even the smallest stone will affect the whole pool's pattern. There is no separateness of existence nor effect. It is a similar concept to Indra's Net in Buddhism.

We have Ur-logs in our own lives – the big ripples, such as love won and lost, illness, relations, betrayal and all the tangles of our human existence.

In the ceremony we are invited to add new Ur-logs (laws) through a pledge or to change our ways or to do things differently. If you have been battling difficulties, the blot ceremony (which is a traditional blessing ceremony) offers a potential seed in laying down another pathway, another event. Ceremony, private or in a group, is a place to activate this change, to make magic happen either as individuals or as a society.

The heart of ceremony is transformation and when done correctly it can offer us a set of new eyes with which to view our relationships, obstacles or community. Central to the wedding ceremony is the community that witnesses the newly-weds. Their love is given protection from those invited and the gods present. Fidelity and trust are granted through the ceremony, with vows and pledges made before those present. The rings exchanged symbolize something that will be unbroken and unchanging, the circle being the image of eternity.

CHAPTER 2

Norse Creation – Myth Cycle

DRINKING THE STARS – CREATION MYTH

Please note, all these myth-cycles are reinterpretations and retellings from the Prose Edda, which include improvisations by the campfire. They have come out from the breath and not the page, landing somewhere between ideas, myth and art.

Before the verdant forests, seas and mountains there was only a first primal anonymity, named Ginnungagap – an apt name for something incomprehensible. There was no existence, nor was there no non-existence. A witch's cauldron where all possibility is contained, the mother of light, the original womb.

Her first born was a flame. Fire is the first, the last, and the most powerful force in all the cosmos, the destroyer of worlds and its creator.

Inside of every flame resides the fire giant Surt who is prophesied to one day burn the heavens. Surt lives in the heart of all flames; all heat and explosions grow from his billows.

At the same time, to the north of the gape, where the fire flakes of Muspelhem couldn't reach, was the opposite realm – the realm of ice. A moon-like opalescent world of wailing and shrieking hurricanes. There in its centre roars the great Hvergelmir and there flows eleven great rivers: the Elivagar. They burst and surge out of Nifelheim and they sometimes collide with the fire flakes of Muspelhem. For eons, these two worlds of fire and ice existed side by side. These are the primordial worlds. When the ice waves of Nifelheim touched the fire flakes of Muspelhem, something started to happen, something took shape.

A being of clay, an androgyne named Ymir: the screamer. The child of fire and ice.

Like all newborns, Ymir screamed into the emptiness with a voice that still rumbles and thunders today in the howling ocean ripped by a hurricane, in every engine, sea wave and storm. This original scream is the heart of every scream since, the sound of all newborns – all our own original mantra. Ymir was neither female nor male.

They roared, starved and craved for sustenance. They were said to have "hug" inside – a spark of consciousness.

They wandered into the ice world. In the gloom, whirlwinds girdled around them.

23

Ymir's hunger was sated by the help of the most forgotten goddess of northern Europe – Holy Audhumla. Audhumla nurtured the first baby. All northern lands suffer from forgetting her. She is without any songs or tributes. The holy cow – blessings to the Brahmans in India keeping her praises alive.

> *'And this prayer of the singer*
> *continually expanding,*
> *Became a cow that was there before*
> *the beginning of the world'*
> – Rig Veda

Audhumla carries a life-giving milk; the milk that she has been giving to all living beings since the beginning. A drop of her memory is still alive in the name of our galaxy, the Milky Way. An older name for our galaxy is the Cow's Lane.

Ymir suckled her teats and then fell asleep. Ymir started to sweat profusely; armpits flooded with sweat.

From the sweat a being called Mimir was born – memory.

The Goddess of Birth and Death was also born from Mimir's body – Bestla. Then more beings were born from under Ymir's feet – strange beings, elves, giants, trolls and the dreaded frost giants.

Audhumla fed all her children. But she also needed sustenance.

She started to lick the ice blocks; she licked until ice started to thaw. A head of a person, named Bure, was revealed in the ice. Just as Ymir had given birth through his armpit, Bure gave birth from his thigh to a son named Bor – the father of the gods.

There in the ice world, there were no stars, only whirlwinds and the roaring of great rivers, Bor wandered many years between the ice blocks. There was a great longing in this heart and one day he met Bestla. In the frozen wilderness, she looked at him with soul-seeking eyes and she became the sovereign queen in his heart, and he the sovereign king in hers – they fell in love. For eons they were joined and Bestla was pregnant. Out there in the ice sheets she screamed and wailed as she gave birth to triplets – Odin, Vile and Ve.

All three sons carried inside of them a dream, with deep imagination of forests, animals, mountains and breaking waves; they dreamed of Middle Earth and our world, and they dreamed of many worlds. They wanted to start to build, to begin to create.

In Nifelheim, each time the brothers started to build something, the giants that were born from the sweat of Ymir broke it down and an enmity grew towards each other. Over time, the giants would break up the brothers' dream-creations of earth and water and scatter them.

This enmity eventually led to the first war of the Universe. A war between chaos and order, creation and destruction.

The sons of Bor took a wandering fire flake from Muspelhem and placed it north of Ginnungagap, today it is called Polaris – the North Star. They built a mill with large grind stones and seven giant maids moved the heavy stones.

The miller was named Mundilfore and he created worlds using the teeth and the bones of the giants that the brothers fought and killed. He helped the gods to shape their creations.

But Odin knew that his largest and most dangerous battle would have to be against the firstborn babe, Ymir – the biggest of all the giants and the most wild.

Upon an ice mountain in Nifelheim they battled, none was a victor at first and for many years they fought. Until one day, Odin (spirit) cut open the throat of Ymir and blood cascaded out of his veins which flooded the whole of Nifelheim, drowning many giants and since then giants would never swim.

The gods took Ymir's body, dismembered it and put it through the world-mill. With the teeth, hair, feet and bones they started to fashion seven worlds:

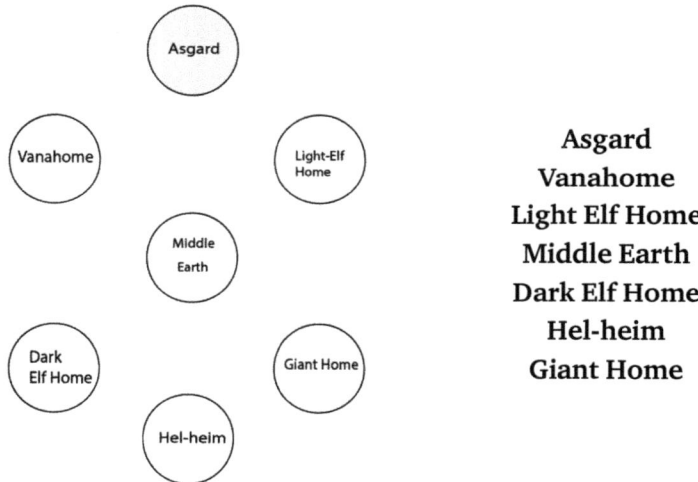

Asgard
Vanahome
Light Elf Home
Middle Earth
Dark Elf Home
Hel-heim
Giant Home

Our world the gods called Midgard – the Middle Earth. Over Middle Earth Ymir's skull was placed as the sky, held up by four dwarves: north, east, south and west – to forever hold it together upon their shoulders.

Ymir's brain is today the floating clouds. Always moving and always thinking – changing like the weather.

His decapitation and the creation of the seven worlds ended the first war between the gods and the giants.

The great miller Mundilfore was proud of his mill and his creations. He boasted that he was the greatest creator over all the worlds; he even challenged Odin himself, but this he did to his regret.

Mundilfore had two beautiful children, Mani (Moon) and Sol (Sun), and they were full of insight and helped their father in setting the courses of the stars as they took more fire flakes from the fires of Muspelhem and placed them across Ginnungagap. As the miller continued to boast of his powers, the gods punished him and stole his children from him (Moon and Sun) and made them ride over the arched heavens on chariots of gold and silver – Sol, the Sun maiden, drives the chariot of the Sun and Mani, the handsome youth, drives the Moon chariot. Since that time, Mani counts the years of trolls, witches and giants and they follow his course because time within the Moon's rays is slow; whereas Sol counts the years of humankind.

Mani performed the same crime as that which was done to his father and he stole two children from a cruel father named Vidfinner.

Vidfinner had sent his two children, Hjuki and Bil, on an impossible quest – they were told to go and look for the mead of magic hidden in a spring-well deep within the mountain. Legends speak of the mead that flows from the iron-veined mountain. One night they succeeded in finding it. They collected as much as they could. Walking carefully, they returned back to their father, trying not to spill a single drop. As they descended the mountainside, a few drops fell to the ground. Mani saw the shimmering liquid and immediately seized the pail of mead and took the children with him to the Moon.

There they are today helping Mani to navigate through the darkness to keep up with the course of Sol (the Sun).

The spots on the Moon's surface are Bil and Hyuki's faces, as they look back towards their distant home. In Mani's keeping there are sharp thorns from old, rooted trees which pierce poets who seek to taste the spilt mead from the Moonchildren, and all those who look at the Moon long enough will feel the melancholy of Hjuki and Bil.

Odin and his brothers were always imagining what the world can become, how they can breathe spirit into it, and with the creation of humankind, Odin exhaled his breath towards the first tree, an elm tree, and a creature emerged from its branches, her eyes were animated and alive, with a waist in the shape of a chalice – she the first woman, the breath of spirit was able to grow within her. Then from an ash tree, another creature was revealed with a clear brow and joyful eyes and a hearty body. He became known as a man.

Trees are humanity's original ancestors.

The night is a goddess who binds the world in dark invisible threads; she loves to take away sorrow and comforts all children who rest in her shadows when Sol sinks into the horizon. High up in the stars, she is wedded to Nagelfare, the god who travels between the stars. Darkness finds delight in water. Water and darkness wedded together and their child was Jord – Earth, she whose body covers the Middle Earth – made of flowering hills and forests – the Goddess of the Earth, Odin's beloved.

She gave birth to a son, Thor: the protector of the Earth and all its creatures.

The Night Goddess also seduced Delling, the Elf of Dawn, and gave him a son called Dagr – Day.

Night rides forth across the sky between every twelve hours on her horse Hrimfaxi. Her son, Day, rides out after on his steed

Skinfaxi – his mane is the luminous thread of light that awakens Middle Earth.

The Second War in the Worlds

When the worlds were created, the gods knew their notions of time and the day and night counted the days for humankind.

The Goddess Freya, a daughter of nature from Vanahome, travelled to the world of the sky gods. Her body was a river, rain, hills and meadows, she spoke of magic in their halls; she spoke of runes and spells which contained all possibilities, she stood lactating milk and she was as naked as a mountain pass, in her tiara there were flowers, each one a key to open the gates of ecstasy, pleasures, desire and beauty. She promised birth and her magic was the most potent of all the worlds.

She was feared.

They called her a dangerous witch, took her and chained her in the halls and cast torches around her to burn her to ashes. When she endured pain, she responded with words of freedom, of chains breaking, of waters cascading.

Bravery wrapped around her – she vanquished all spells.

Then in the hall she sang a spell in reprisal to the rising flames around her:

> *"Rich in nature is the old magic's treasure*
> *A sweet soul does not give up*
> *Even when the world is turned to ashes*
> *I return burnished in gold, as Goldwinde*
> *I have been through the fire yet I come alive*
> *through these flames I will survive!"*

When the flames engulfed her body, she shone like a burning Sun in the hall.

Each time more torches were cast onto her, her light burnt brighter. The fire was mending her and shaping her. From within the flames, she sang ancient runes that echoed in the halls, she gave a song of golden magical loquaciousness, a high falsetto voice mixed with smoky air in the halls. Her beauty was uncontaminated and she was naked as the waves in the sea. All her clothes had burnt to cinders and her only remaining garment was now the girdle of emotion, lined with the dream of harvest and birth upon her waist. She was alive with feeling, a bright pulse of sentience, her eyes were deep rays of light in the darkest sea and her hair flowed and oscillated above the flames. When her song was flung out into the air, the Moon was in her command, magic entered the hall. Darkness was transformed into the mother of light as she weaved the thread of fate between the gods and the Vanir.

Nobody could stop her spell-songs as they broke her chains and in the likeness of a hawk, she fled into the skies above.

When the great Vanir Lord Frey himself heard about her treatment, a council was called for reprisal and justice. Bird messengers were sent between the worlds and a great concourse gathered where the seven rivers met.

The Vanir spoke before the Aesir, saying: "Our daughter was mistreated at the hands of your warriors; burnt and chained – a grievous crime. We seek to settle this grief and demand justice."

They responded:

"She passed unnoticed into Valhalla through sorcery, this is forbidden."

"Hear you not my words? Will you not grant what we ask of you?"

The Aesir remained silent.

More words of power and threats of reprisals were exchanged until a spear was cast over the heads of the Vanir, symbolizing war. This was the first war since Odin and Ymir had fought on the plains of Nifelheim and the beginning of the conflict between the Sky Gods and the Spirits of Nature.

The conflict lasted for many ages. Forests were burnt down, and the land was destroyed. The World Tree itself, Yggdrasil, was weakened; vows broken, turmoil everywhere, the dreams of a future forgotten. Warriors from both sides yearned for glory and victory, before they fell in their own blood, and sorcerers from both sides expired in spell-flames.

In the ashes, both sides recognized that there could never be a winner.

But then, one day, a truce was agreed.

Weaponless upon the glittering fields of Hel, on the ninth day of the waxing moon, the Aesir and Vanir gathered for a ritual of reconciliation.

All were gathered when the Wolf God spoke:

"Powerful are the spells that bind us in war and destruction. We are thirsty to renew our vows; we seek a firm and sacred knot of reconciliation between us. We wish for the currents of our fates to bend. May we have a worthier future."

Frey answered: "Look at the withered leaves on the World Tree and the destruction of the gardens and groves of your halls – let's put an end to this unsightly war."

When those words were spoken, all bent in front of the sorrows of the past, and the tears that were shed were collected in a basket of flowers. Once the tears ceased and were undisturbed by doubt or fear, a reconciliation was sanctioned.

The vat contained tears and spit from both sides, and it started to shimmer like a silver shield. Potent was the magic.

The gods and the Vanir didn't want to pour out the tears on the ground and watch them dissolve. Instead, they created a being from this holy liquid. The time of flowers had returned and out of the vat a new leader was born, uniting Sky Gods and Nature Spirits – his name was Kvasir, the emergent wisdom.

Kvasir spoke:

"Hear me, do not let the flames of anger leap and devour. With wisdom and guidance, do not pluck the young from the Tree of Life before their time. Give up your thoughts of injuring the other. In the presence of the gods of the nine realms, let us reconcile the high heavens and the worlds beneath. Cry out with wild prayers for love to endure. May our words be open for all to see. This is my decree."

With those words, reconciliation was final between the warring tribes.

The Aesir sent two of their leaders to live with the Vanir tribe – long-legged Aesir called Honir and Mimir. Mimir was one of the first born from the race of giants. Memory, his counsel, was always sought in matters of health and knowledge.

Much was sung about Kvasir when he walked the nine worlds and a story of bloodshed followed.

THE RUNES OF CREATION

The etymology of the word "rune" means: "to carve" or "to cut". In Low German, the word is "raunen". As the runes were cut and carved into wood, metal or stone, the word "rune" was analogous to the rune letters themselves. In Old English, "writing" comes from "wrītan"; which originally meant to scratch lines or symbols onto wood or stone.

The runic forms and shapes varied according to the materials. For example, runes carved into wood had more straight lines than the more rounded rune shapes inscribed into granite.

The word rune also means: "mystery, secret or whisper."

In northern Europe, the runes were actively used for a thousand years approximately between the ages of 150 CE to 1100 CE and, like any writing system, they were used as a reliable form of information storage and as a verbal representation – as signs.

After 1100 CE they were replaced by the Latin writing system with the incoming colonization of Rome.

Magical Symbolism

When we study the runes and the runic objects, however, we do not only come across linguistic patterns representing practical information, such as accounts of dates and names, we also come across "non-linguistic" inscriptions which represent magical symbolism and incantations of protections, blessings or curses. The most famous example is the rune trio ALU. This trio is seen carved in brooches and magical bracteate (bracteates are thin single-sided gold discs worn as jewellery in northern Europe during the Iron Age); the motifs on the discs are of northern mythology with icons giving protection.

Inscribing weapons and tools with runes was a widespread magical practice.

Reading the Poetic Edda, Sigrdrífumál mentions "victory runes" to be carved on a sword, "some on the grasp and some on the inlay, and name Tyr twice."

These examples reveal that the runes contained in themselves an old magical form and tradition – each rune had a potent symbolic meaning and a purpose. But sadly, as the runic writing faded away, so did its magical use and today we only have a few echoes left from this "thousand-year-long" history.

Here I am presenting an imaginary journey through the great cosmos and the creation myth and how we can bestow the runes an association and a symbolic aliveness through this story.

Ginnungagap

We begin with the "first cause" – which is infinity and emptiness. It is the place which has "neither existence nor non-existence" – not up, no down. It is known as Ginnungagap – the empty void.

A "magically charged void" because all possibilities are born from there. We can never know Ginnungagap, as it is our "first cause" – to know it would be like lifting oneself off the ground or being able to see your own eyes without a mirror – the emptiness refers to our very first inner nature. It is the ultimate non-duality.

The beginning. The rune UR – ᚾ reflects this, the origin or emptiness. The symbol is two cow horns after the gigantic cow named Audhumla "void, darkness". The origin of the Universe. This is closely connected to the sacred cows of the Hindu tradition as the "Mother" and the northern customs have the Indo-European religion as one of their roots.

In India, the Earth Goddess Prithvi had the form of a cow, she was known to bring growth to crops and end famines. Kamadhenu, depicted as the miraculous "Cow of Plenty," represents this sacred cow. Here, the heavenly cow feeds the giant Ymir from whence all life comes.

Cows are the real wet nurses of millions of people around the world. The Diwali celebration, the main festival in India, is connected to the veneration and worship of cows as they bring livelihood and protection.

The cow's milk which gives Ymir consciousness is seen as the Milky Way. An ancient name for the Milky Way is the "Cow's Lane". The Rig Veda has a prayer for Audhumla, the Mother of Time and of the gods.

> *"And this prayer of the singer*
> *continually expanding,*
> *Became a cow that was there before*
> *the beginning of the world."*

Fire and Ice

Here we enter the dual Universe, the ups and the downs, the back and forth, the opposites.

Fire is the first being, and all living things are tempered by fire, and are born and destroyed through fire. Our own self-discovery comes from fire; it was the first "being" in the Universe. In the immemorial times when fire was first experienced, it was our first veneration. Fire was also to be feared as it ripped through the land. In the Norse creation myth, we meet the fire giant Surt – the destroyer. His sword shall cleave the heavens at the end of time.

But the giant Surt also brings us a priceless gift in fire and all its uses in discovery, security, and transformations – be it food or metal.

Ice

The ice world is a cold and uninhabitable wasteland. Here we have the opposite of the world of fire. The ice world is a symbol of frozen patience and long-awaited potential. The world of ice has yet to thaw and to break loose its life-giving waters. Ice and fire exist here as two dual forces.

Ymir the Giant

The roaring babe, the primordial being made of clay. Energy wrought into form. Born from the opposites, an androgyn, ungainly, misshapen, his feet were the size of galaxies. The gods killed him in an epic battle. They create the world from him – bones become rocky outcroppings, teeth become gravel and boulders, flesh becomes the earth. Ymir represents a taming of something coming forth from chaos and made into order.

We see the killing of Ymir when the oxen are tamed and harnessed to plough the fields, we see it when we order our streets and our cities – this is a necessary act – but the feud between the giants and the gods never ends after this killing. The gods will pay with their own lives at the end of the world, when order stops and chaos again takes over; it is a cyclical pattern that never ends. The Universe goes back and forth between chaos and order. Here we also see life being born through death – which is a constant recurrence in nature.

Ymir's rune is THURS – Þ and symbolizes the primitive creative energy manifested, out of control and chaos.

The Gods

The gods are the embodiment of the natural laws and powers, which keeps the Sun and the Moon turning correctly and protects from the chaos of the giants. They are the ones who battle the cosmic struggle to maintain order. The Aesir is what the Anglo-Saxon would call the "Ese" – the rafters that uphold the mead hall, the ordered cosmos that provided a roof over our heads.

Audhumla licked on salt stones to keep herself alive and from them the first God of the Aesir was born. He was noble and beautiful; his name was Bure – the first of the Aesir. There followed more beings – Bure had a son named Bor and took for his wife Bestla, who gave birth to Odin (spirit), Ve and Vile. The first Aesir killed the giant Ymir, or (in a translation of mythos) subordinated the raw energy and created the manifest Universe. This is symbolized by the rune ASS – ᚨ.

Next is REID – ᚱ, it stands for order and control of the four directions and the elements. REID is Thor's rune and Thor is the restorer of the cosmic order and REID is linked with the enlightened thunderbolt. REID is also movement and we get direction – and so the first phase of the creation story is done. This rune holds up the four directions in the world. Within the Mithraic cult, the wagon symbolized the holy four-horse carriage, the symbol of the four elements.

From the lightning we get fire, KEN – ‹, which is connected to the fire realm and is a spiritual and creative energy. Here we get the "K" sound. We see this rune in the Anglo-Saxon runesong with the name Cen, a word that means "torch". In German – Kien. The torch is a symbol for fire and light. In the Greek script we have the fifth letter "E" called Eos (morning blush) – linked to light, and the old Greek word for "light", Fos, has also been called "torch".

Fire has its disciples: the smith, potter, alchemist, metallurgist and the witch. At the heart of all their work is transformation. Death and birth are both present as wildfire sweeps over the forests, for green shoots will inevitably rise from the scorched earth. The intensity of Freya's burning bestows a purified residue in the end, what remains is the sheer power of her words and beauty – the outer layers are burned off to expose the core of her vital essence as the great Goddess of the Nine Worlds.

Fire has built all of our civilizations – it's the source of our industry. Psychological fire is the same, with all the emotional constellations: urges, instincts and desires. All of this burns inside us as alchemical flames, the energy it generates expresses elements of our subconscious and our deep motivations for selfhood, spiritual and philosophical insight.

In the beginning of the Rig Veda, the indefinite being, Prajapati (whose name is a pronoun, KA, meaning: "who?"), created fire and this fire terrified the gods. They could only come near it if they wrapped themselves up in sacred poetic metres. The poetic metre is the mantle the gods have to wear when approaching this original fire. The fire cannot be stared at directly.

Why are words important? Everything that exists (according to the Rig Veda) is suffused with two powers: Mind (Manas) and Word (Vac) – and both are equals. The mind is harnessed and saddled like a horse through words; this idea is the essence of mantra singing and the sacred syllable of AUM. Comparatively, this can also be seen as the essence of rune-magical practice – just like the mantra of the Vedas, when we sing the rune "galder" we open new worlds to harness parts of our minds. When you sing the galder of the rune KEN, you begin to access this alchemical fire within.

✕ – GIFU marks the four directions and the symbol for a centre of our lives and the Universe, and its meaning is harmony and balance. GIFU means gift. Here we are in the reciprocal aspect of giving and receiving, the balance of offerings. The essence of the offering and answering the question: "what do you want and how much are you prepared to pay?" The notion of sacrifice being a deferred quality, whereby we give ourselves to an activity (which we may not like to do) in the present moment to obtain a result in the imaginative future.

> *"Never to pray is better*
> *than too many offerings,*
> *the one who gives wants something in return.*
> *Never to Seidr is better*
> *than too much prophecy.*
> *This the one-eyed carved*
> *in the morning of time*
> *when he returned."*
> Havamal, Stanza 145
> (translated by Author).

WYNJA – ᛈ is the rune of happiness and joy in creation.

ᚺ – HAGAL is the bridge between the worlds, the rainbow way – the realm of Heimdall, the watcher and listener.

With ᛏ – NAUD, the goddesses of fate enter the picture, bringing notions of time and our personal needs; the rune itself means "need".

Through the progression of time, past, present and future, the Norns offer creation its original structure.

ᛁ – ISS represents structure, but also Nifelheim and the forming of the power of ice. A rune which points to stillness within us – an excellent glyph for meditation and slowing down.

Once we reach the rune ᛃ – JARA, we come to our world. JARA stands for the seasons and the sacred marriage. Thereafter, we have the runes from the mineral kingdom, ᛈ – PETRA; the vegetable kingdom ᛇ – EOH; and the animal kingdom ALGIZ – ᛉ. Then we have SOL – ᛋ, the Sun, which is the material aspect to the ᚲ – KEN rune. Then man ᛏ – TYR and woman ᛒ – BJARKA. Mankind enters the creation from the trees ash and elm.

With the rune EHWAZ – ᛖ, we are in a state of flux and movement in between worlds and states; and in ᛗ – MADR, we have a balanced person. With LAGUZ – ᛚ, the water element is flowing in the rivers and oceans.

ᛜ – ING stands in relation to the God Ing, the God of the Angles, the people of Ing. Ing is the God of Love and Fertility. We reach the ancestral lines of ᛟ – ODAL, representing tradition, culture, forefathers and all the earlier incarnations – everything that makes us who we are today.

In ᛗ – DAGAZ is the alchemical metamorphosis of creation, from a caterpillar to a butterfly, from an egg to a hatchling, and learning to fly out of the nest and towards ᚠ – FEH, where we reach the completeness of the circle of creation, the totality, the hearth-fire – our spiritual home.

Creation is complete.

CHAPTER 3

Yggdrasil – Remembering

REMEMBERINGS: THE GREAT TREE – YGGDRASIL

At the centre of all the worlds and of all of creation stands Yggdrasil – the Tree of Life.

When Odin hung, speared, for nine days on the World Tree, he uttered the words that he had "sacrificed himself onto himself." This stanza gives us a description of the unity existing between the Godhead and the tree in the myths. To emphasize this connection, we find in Old English the word treow, which means both "tree" and "truth".

Etymologically, then, truth and tree grow out of the same root

Subsequently, in the Norse creation myth, man and woman originated from trees. We are all the sons and daughters of the ash and elm trees – the first man was called Ask, born from the ash; and the first woman Embla, born from the elm. Their oxygen offers us the primordial conditions for life. Ask and Embla sprouted from Yggdrasil's acorns, and so it is that every human being springs from the fruit of Yggdrasil, then to be collected by two storks, which bring them to their longing mothers-to-be. In Scandinavian folklore, they say that children are born through the knot holes in the trunks of pine trees, which is another version of the same myth.

Artur Lundkvist is one of Swedish literature's greatest tree worshippers. Following a reflection on trees and forests, he writes:

> "... in every human there is a tree, and in every tree there is a human, I feel this, the tree wanders inside a human being, and the human being is caught in the tree ... I serenade the forests, the forest sea is the second sea on earth, the sea in which man wanders. The forests work in silence, fulfilling nature's mighty work; working with the winds, cleaning the air, mitigating the climate, forming soil, preserving all our essentials without wearing them out."

People represented Yggdrasil by planting what was called a "care-tree", or "guardian tree" in the centre of the homestead. It was a miniature version of Yggdrasil, and a stately landmark in the courtyard. The care-tree was a figurative expression of the interdependence of the world around us. It had a soul which followed the lives of those who grew up under its shadow and boughs. If the care-tree had witnessed many families growing up, the relationship between the tree and the family would have strengthened – this relationship was known to be private and confidential within the family line. Many such care-trees can still be seen in Scandinavia. I would argue that this is the origin of the Christmas tree. We unknowingly bring the World Tree into our home every winter solstice.

We also gain an understanding from the old vellum scripts that the World Tree is not a transcendental entity beyond time and space; rather, it is alive, organic, fragile and strong. The fragility of Yggdrasil is always a concern to the gods. There is a dragon called the Bane Biter who bites into its deepest roots.

There are also other animals that assail the Tree: four deer feed from the branches, and their names are Dain, Dvalin, Duneyr and Duratro. Dain and Dvalin are described as if they are "dead" or "living with indifference, living in a mist."

Two animals stand on the roof of Valhalla (the abode of the gods) – the goat Heidrun and the deer Eiktyrner, and they feed from the branches too – but they give back gifts to the Tree. The goat offers mead and the deer pours water from its antlers into the roots. They are both said to live in balance with the Tree.

The World Tree is connected with our own creation, preservation and destruction. It teaches us that trees are bound to the fate of the world.

It is up to us to care for our past, to remember that which we have lost, and also to celebrate the flowering world, the present moment, whilst reaching forward to a possible future – a future that we can all shape together.

OUR SEVEN SOULS

A Northern Soul Perception
The polytheistic mindset of northern Europe had perceptions of self which was closer to the idea of "psyche" – which is a nuanced, complex and polysensory notion of the self.

Folklorists studying the notion of self-hood in the sagas and folktales have rediscovered these many different aspects to the self, this material is ambiguous and examples can sometimes overlap with each other. It is written to be in the service of the imagination and not to be seen as a single, unified system. Instead, we see an overview of these concepts across the folkloric material, which enables us to gain some fascinating insights:

The Hug

The first "self-entity" we read about is called "hug" – it can be translated as something that drives our thoughts, desires and emotions. The hug is part of the personality of the person. Everyone carries a hug (note also that Hugin is one of the ravens that sit on Odin's shoulder, where he is personified as "thought").

Our hug helps us through the many challenges we confront in our lives. But our hug can also be stolen or weakened: if our desire is weak, or the mood is low, then you may have been "hug-stolen".

This was usually blamed on a supernatural entity that had come and fed on your thoughts and desires – they were known as hug-biters. When your will-power is low, it can be an indication that your hug has been compromised or attacked. Depression, in this context, can be seen as being a major "hug-thief". With the help of folk magic and other cunning means, you can try to empower the hug of a person. The conscious desire to change or transform the hug can be seen as the basis for northern magic.

It was believed, and it still is believed in many parts of Scandinavia, that the hug can change both animate and inanimate objects. Most of the descriptions about the changes of a hug are collected in the folktales (see "Nordic Folklore: Recent Studies, edited by Reimund Kvideland and Henning K. Sehmsdorf).

Hug-Ham

The hug is able to wander outside of the body. When it is outside of the body then it activates another part of us called the "ham". The ham, in occult studies and practices, would be associated with the astral body. When both hug and ham are linked, we have a "hug-ham". According to folklorist Bente G. Alver, there can be three shapes to the hug-ham:

- *The shape of the person*
- *The shape of an animal*
- *An abstract shape, mist or light*

The hug-ham can go on many adventures, both within our imaginations and outside in the "real" world. For those of you who have experienced trance and journeying or strong mind-alterations, those would be experiences of taking on the shape of the hug-ham. Similar to many shamanic traditions around the world, a hug-ham can perform a magic flight to accomplish something, or to find something that is lost, to access knowledge, open portals, communicate with the spirits – this hug-ham transformation can be unconsciously created, or it can also be vital and conscious.

When it is conscious and directed it becomes witchcraft. The witch being the master at exercising her hug-ham travels in the shape of various animals, or any other animate shapes. Witches differ from most in that they have the capacity to use their hug-ham at will. Most of us who have experienced the sensations of leaving our bodies and travelling into other realms do so often. Without the capacity to navigate with the hug-ham, we end up being tossed between the waves in the astral ocean. Many experience this when in highly altered states.

The ability to navigate your hug and to use it at will requires practice and is a gift from the gods – such travelling is not meant to be for all, it was done by few of those that were called for such work.

The Fylgja

The "fylgja" is another part of the self which can be viewed as the equivalent of the "totem animal" or "spirit animal" that exists all across the world. The word fylgja means "to accompany" – it is the same word as the "fetch" in Irish folklore.

In the sagas, the fylgjur take on the shape and character of their owners – a loud and burly man would be associated with a bear; or a doe-eyed girl with a fawn; a crafty person with a fox. Fylgjur accompany you at birth and death. They are not controllable as the hug-self is, the fylgjur have an independent will.

In the larger mythic imagination, animal powers bring forth the original instruction about the purpose of your life; they know the answer to the question: why are you here? They are sometimes depicted across cultures as sitting on the branches of the World Tree, calling out the reasons for your birth into the material world and giving instructions. The trouble is, the amniotic birth goes through the "great waters of forgetting" – we forget the original instructions and then spend most our lives trying to find them again.

One remarkable insight about the fylgja is its role in dreams. In folkloric studies this has been called the "dream-self" at times. When your body is rested and asleep, your fylgja leaves and goes out into the nine worlds – flying, running on four legs, or swimming in the sea. The experiences that the fylgja is having whilst it is travelling translates directly as your own dreaming self.

The dreams you have at night is the experience the fylgja is having as it leaves your body when you are asleep. When you wake, the fylgja comes back into your body and your dreams have been the fylgja's experience of the world. The fylgja is also described as the dreaming soul.

The Ward

Another important part of the self is the "ward". Ward comes from the word Vård in Swedish. The ward is regarded as a memory entity which stays behind in the places where people have died. In the Eddas, Odin is often out there bargaining with the ward of a witch, trying to get information. Accessing the information of the ward can be seen as the original form of necromancy. When we access the ward of a person, we access their memory and gain important information about that person's life. Anyone who has gone to the graves of ancestors or loved-ones often feels the compulsion to speak out loud as the presence of their ward can be strong. In the large grave mounds this can be especially

48

powerful and overwhelming. From experience and speaking with other people, the ward is particularly raised and present when we speak of stories associated with place. If the memory is strong enough, the ward can be beheld and its appearance mistaken for a ghost.

The Ond

Another part of the multi-self is the "ond". Closely associated with the "force" of Odin or the Odic force. This part of the self was studied in detail by Baron Carl von Reichenbach in 1845. Von Reichenbach wanted to develop scientific proof for a universal life force; like the Asian "chi" or "prana" – he experimented on people where they would be in total darkness to try and "see" their ond. Through his practice he claimed that a third of the population could see this phenomenon.

Since then, these practices remain in the occult community, particularly in the yoga and martial art practices, where you can sense the ond in yourself or in other people. Creating heat through the hands is one such example and other such phenomena can be regarded as ond energy.

Those people can carry a high amount of ond energy and can be suited to heal through touch.

Lik

As the "ham" represents the astral shape, the "lik" represents the physical shape of the body. Arms, legs, feet, hands and head. The body is the Middle Earth, and all the elements give it its life.

Symbolism associated with the body:

Head: Thinking
Hair: Strength
Eyes: Perception
Nose: Breath
Mouth: Communication
Tongue: Taste
Ears: Sound
Face: Image
Neck: Balance
Heart: Emotions

With these symbols you can readily see where there are issues to work with. It is easy to miss underlying causes, symbols reveal them. For example, headaches or migraines relate to the head, which in turn is the "thinking" part of the body. What does doubt represent, or envy? It is mentioned in folktales that envy can have a detrimental effect on someone, it can damage the person's hug; for example, next time you have a headache, try and follow it to the source if you can. If your life has been out of balance, how is that affecting your neck? If you have spent a long time inside working, or feeling stuck, what does that do to the nose? These are perceptions that relate to our stresses and joys – by having different emotions, they affect part of the body – this is just common folk-sense, belonging to the folk-medicine, but it is often overlooked.

The sensations in your body, or where your weaknesses and strengths lie, hold information that can reveal insights when you see yourself being made with many different parts.

Minni

Minni means memory – the memories you carry in your life can have a great effect on your present. Before the Sun God comes out to evaporate the past, Urd collects this memory-water and pours it into her well: the Well of Memory.

The dew water is named Aurr. Although the Sun God always shines in the present, Urd finds our memories too precious and keeps them safe. If the past is discarded, memories forgotten, the well will not feed the roots, and if Yggdrasil is not watered by our memories, then the Tree of Life withers and loses its vitality.

In the centre of Urd's well there are two sacred swans, which form a heart shape with their long necks when facing each other, creating the fertility symbol of the God Frey (the God of Love and Fertility). Love arises from this holy well. In esoteric practice we can also map these seven self-perceptions into runic associations or personal sigils, to learn more about them and to discover what we need to develop in ourselves.

To be in harmony with all seven parts is to be in health spiritually and psychologically. Often, we find some parts easier to strengthen than others. Finding out which one we need to be working on requires insight and self-reflection and the rune-cast can sometimes guide us in this discovery.

More aspects of the self-found in the lore:

Od

Od is having the capacity to experience forms of consciousness that are radically unlike our normal forms of consciousness – the English word of something being "odd" comes from this Old Norse word.

Hamingja

The totality of all the aspects of the souls is the link between the hamr and the fylgja in this word. Usually, the kings and queens of the land would carry strong hamingja. Those who have a strong hamingja can bless the community and the land.

Having a strong hamingja is the elder hood. It denotes someone who has walked through all the worlds and has had many lived experiences. The fylgja (totem animal) would be the shield mark of such a person. The most common totemic representations in the Norse world are ravens, eagles, wolves, boars and bears.

Indeed, the raven and the wolf are seen as the ancient symbols of the valkyries. The valkyries' function was to bring the warriors back to the ancestors after battle. The raven and wolf later on transformed into shield maidens who ride horses, the "choosers of the slain." In the Viking Age, they were depicted as being swans originally.

Megin – (prana/chi in the East) denotes magical power, it is located below the navel. Everything has megin – plants, stones, trees, rivers and more.

Hamingja Practice

The emotional and thinking realm of the hug can be enlivened and enhanced by investigating our emotional journeys and reflections; the arts can be a helpful vehicle here – painting, poetry and music. Looking for that part which can ventilate and expand your inner feelings and thoughts. If you are overthinking and your hug feels weakened, then look for ways where you are able to write down your thoughts and give yourself the time to look at them properly. It may be helpful to remember and to see the ebb and flow of your thinking – when is it most active? What time of the day are you more mentally at ease? What aesthetics around you gives you a sense of well-being?

Gratitude can be a relief from the stresses of overthinking. For your "ond" being out in the natural world with its fragrance and sound offers the opportunity to surrender to life and its currents and form, allowing yourself to experience the divine ecstatic nature which is life and to also nourish the awareness that this is a force you readily tap into. Body practices for strengthening the "lik" can be swimming in water, eating, massage and exercise. What happens when you take care of the physical (lik), does it translate and link it also to the spiritual (ond)? Or is it vice-versa? Experiment and find out what works.

Work with the idea of all the seven parts of yourself being part of the great Tree and learn to identify the part that feels vulnerable or more difficult to approach. Usually where the difficulty is, is also where the greatest opportunities for development lie.

CHAPTER 4

Mead of Poetry – Myth Cycle

THE SECOND CREATION MYTH CYCLE: THE MEAD OF POETRY

Kvasir, the son of gods' tears and spit, travelled into all the nine worlds and even through to the outer regions of the giants, where he taught poetry and skill with rhetoric. He could answer every question anyone asked him. He gave instructions and was received well everywhere he went. One day, two dwarf-smiths named Fjalar and Galarr prepared a dinner for him in a golden dungeon deep in the ground where they lived. Into the stew they had thrown clusters of deadly nightshade flower petals. When Kvasir had eaten only a morsel, he instantly died. The dwarves drained all his blood into two large bronze vats, named Son and Bodn, and then proceeded to pour it all into a large kettle called Odrerir (the ecstasy-giver), where they mixed potent honey with his blood. Kvasir's bones were buried deep in the mountain and will one day be retrieved by a god.

It was known across the worlds that anyone who would ever drink of the blood of Kvasir would become a great poet and scholar and would learn all the knowledge that the world has to offer, for in his blood was the wisdom of all. For Fjalar and Galarr however, their lot was cursed – instead, insatiable madness and lust for gold was their award.

Kvasir had been deeply loved by all and his blood and tombstone belonged in the heavens of Asgard, not down and forgotten in the dungeons of greed. The giants first heard about the disappearance of Kvasir from the Spirit of the Mountain, and one giant named Gillingr and his wife went to visit both dwarves.

"I have heard that Kvasir was last seen in your abode, is this right?" Asked Gillingr as he stood before their oak doors. "He did and he was too wise for his own good." Fjalar responded. The dwarves worried about the giant's curiosity and thought they must be rid of him in case he discovered the liquid treasures. They told the giant, "We are going out fishing for our dinner, if you join us in the boat we can eat together." Gillingr agreed to join them, reluctantly – ever since the great floods in the beginning of time, giants have been weary of Ymir's blood, the ocean.

Their boat heaved in the waves and the wind lashed a grey assault onto the sullen cliffs. As they rowed further and further away from the shore, the sea started to boom in displeasure, the waves splashed on their faces. One breaking after another, their boat keeled and tilted. As Galarr took up his oar and he lifted it above his head and smacked it over Gillingr's head, surprising him from the back, the oar did not hurt his skull, instead he lost his balance and he fell into the water. The two dwarves left him to drown.

His wife, when she heard the news, uprooted boulders from her lamenting, her eyes soul-scalding, she wanted to smite anyone nearby. Fjalar and Galarr managed to hide far into the dungeon, they feared that she would suspect them. The dungeons in the mountain protected them for a time.

In their continuing madness, the dwarves hid in their deepest chambers and there they continuously added more honey and herbs to Kvasir's blood, making it more potent. The vats and the kettle hissed and cooked, spells were cast and muttered over the vat and the fire was kept white hot with their great bellows. Each time they tasted the sprite-elixir, they were overcome with more cunning and more plotting – the curse of their greed drove them onwards. Until, one day, Suttungr (the son of Gillingr) arrived before their doors, but he did not knock, instead he tore down the granite rocks, crushing everything that stood in his way with his bare hands. He ripped apart the mountain until he found the dwarves, where he took them by their hair and walked them out to the frothy sea. After he'd put them on a cliff, Fjalar pleaded, "Don't kill us, we are working with the water of life, the mead of inspiration, that which makes us wise and gives us knowledge. Our work is not finished, please do not take our lives, I beg you, spare us. We can make a deal, if you spare our lives, you can have the mead of inspiration, the very blood of Kvasir."

To this Suttungr agreed.

The dwarves' lives ended in the cold mountains, where they suffered a lonely and painful old age, whimpering at their inevitable doom inside their silenced dungeons.

Suttungr took the vats and the kettle and brought it home, he kept it safe, deep into his hillside. His daughter Gunnlod watched over them day and night. She would sit in front of a bronze shield and comb her hair, reflecting her beauty; she was transfixed by her own allure and waited patiently for a suitor to arrive.

Odin sat on his throne and he could see into many secrets of the nine worlds and hear from his ravens about the fate of Kvasir. The blood of Kvasir belonged to the Aesir and the Vanir, Kvasir was the son of their pledges of peace, it was not right for it to be in the possession of giants. Filled with rage, he saddled his horse. Sleipnir shot out like a hawk across the sky. Odin travelled day and night, until he arrived in the land of the giants. Through cunning alone, he was going to take the mead of inspiration back to Valhalla, to take the blood back to those who had formed Kvasir, for the blood would nourish and give wisdom until the end of days.

Odin decided to travel to the farmstead of Suttungr's brother, Baugi. When he arrived, he came upon nine thrall giants mowing hay. The metal on their scythes had gone blunt and they had worked for days without much progress, their brows sweating under a fierce sun. The Terrible One approached them and asked them if they wanted their scythes to be sharpened. They said yes, and from his belt he took out a whetstone and started to sharpen the scythes, they cut the grass and the work took seconds rather than hours to complete. They asked to buy the whetstone from him, but Odin quoted it as priceless, so they demanded it from him, ready to pay the price. Then, instead of selling it to them, he cast the whetstone high up in the air and as it dropped, all of them followed its fall into the long grass. As it lay there, they all ran for it and when they tried to grasp it some of them were pushed to the side, others were cut by someone's scythe, and their greed turned to violence. They started to strike each other with their sharp scythes, one cut at first, then a second, which drew blood, but when a third cut out a crimson fountain, the fight turned into a frenzy with terrible screeching from the blades and a flurry of activity like seabirds fighting for a morsel of meat. Before long, there was no single winner, for all of them had fallen before the newly sharpened blades of the deadly scythes.

When Baugi found them, he could see that they had all killed each other. He grieved over his condition and the fate of his thralls, as he would have no chance of finding other workmen and thus the wheat would remain in the fields. As he was lamenting the fate of his farm, Odin approached him and introduced himself as Bolverk. He said he would work and harvest the wheat, save the farm, and do the same work as nine giant thralls. "What price do you demand for such an undertaking?" asked Baugi. Odin replied, "Just one drink of Suttungr's Mead from the mountain." Baugi laughed, "You are asking two impossible tasks, nobody can access the chamber in the mountain, and there is no god or giant alive who alone can harvest the large golden fields of Jotunhem." Baugi turned his back and started to walk away, "Are you not willing to give me a chance?" Baugi turned around and offered him his scythe. "If you can cut this field of hay in one day, then I will believe you."

Bolverk sharpened his scythe and started to cut the hay, he quickly completed the entire stretch of the field, a job which should have taken days he did in an instant. He was taken on as a labourer and over the late summer and autumn all the work was done with the utmost speed and quality, and so the farm thrived.

By the end of the autumn period, when all the harvest and work had been completed, Bolverk asked Braugi about their deal and whether he could now have one sip of the mead held by his brother Suttungr. Braugi told him that they would go together the next morning and seek out his brother under the mountain and ask him for a drop of the mead. The journey was long, away from the grasslands and up and across giant territories which were covered with silent sky-spearing mountains that loomed over them as they walked.

Then in the distance they saw Suttungr's mountain. There a cunning mist had started to girdle around its crown. As they approached they could make out a large black hole – the entrance to Suttungr's halls. Standing in front of his entrance, Braugi bellowed for his brother, causing freezing white boulders to surge and crumble down the mountainside. A moment passed and Suttungr stood in front of his entrance.

"Dear brother, I made a bargain with this man called Bolverk to have a sip of the mead, if he could harvest the fields with the strength of nine giant thralls, this he did. He has helped the farm, so can he receive just one sip?"

Suttungr thundered, "NO! The mead is not to be touched by man, giants, elves or gods. It belongs to our family only; the answer is no! Get on your way, and do not waste my time by coming here as beggars." He walked back into the dark cave.

Braugi was uncomfortable with how he had fallen short in his promise to offer a drop of mead. Bolverk asked if he was prepared to try a more scheming way of getting the mead, and Braugi agreed.

They walked and clutched at the elbow of the mountain as they made progress through the bone-white snow. Bolverk stopped and started to push the snow aside to get down to the mountain-granite, then he took a small drill called Rati. Rati could bite into anything. With that, Bolverk asked Braugi to start to drill into the mountainside with all his strength. Rati bit further and deeper into the side of the mountain. "Try and blow into the hole and see if we are through yet," said Bolverk. Braugi blew into the hole but the dust flew out to his face, meaning the mountain had not been penetrated fully. Braugi tried again with all the strength he could muster. When Bolverk asked for the third time, the dust from the granite flew inwards, which was a sign that they had reached into the mountain halls. Then Bolverk disappeared, he was gone, Braugi looked around. Then he caught only a glimpse of a glittering silver serpent that had slid into the hole of the mountain. Bolverk was not who he said he was.

Now well inside the mountain, Odin slithered inside a large rough-hewn chamber. Then he wound his way toward a bronze-lit room where beautiful Gunnlod was sitting facing her bronze shields. Next to her were rippling silken tapestries woven in liquid all inside the large vats, full of colour and prismatic reflections. She was a queenly figure with crescent shaped eyebrows and blossom-pink lips. Odin transformed into a god and met her gaze, full of magnetism, wizard dust whirling around him, and he carried such strong sorcery that Gunnlod was seduced instantly. She had found her suitor, whom she had longed for in the lonely tomb-silence of the mountain. For three days they lay together encased in each other's limbs, her heart was full of joy and so she forgot her responsibilities. When Odin asked if he could quench his thirst a little from the mead in the vats, she offered him kindly to take only three small sips. Odin walked towards the soul-water and there he cupped his hands and drank every drop out of the three large vats, Odrerir, Bodn and Son. Gunnlod witnessed him standing there having just drained her father's mead.

Then his head and body transformed into a golden eagle, he uttered that their child would be the first poet in the world – Bragi. He flew out of her chamber, through the inner dungeons and out into the polar-blue sky. When Suttungr heard the scream of Gunnlod, he understood he had been robbed by a powerful sorcerer. He took himself an eagle shape and followed after Odin in the skies. For days the chase was maintained, both flew out of the lands of giants altogether and into the realms of the Aesir.

The gods on their ramparts could see the two eagles flying towards them, one in flight and the other in a furious chase. Straight away they set out the large vats as Odin had instructed them to, awaiting their great eagle to return to Asgard. He swooped down and surged up in the wind currents. Ever-present on his tail was Suttungr, who could almost nip his tail feathers. Odin had but one option to shake off his pursuer. He sent some mead out from his backside which splashed horribly into the face of Suttungr. Some of this mead was caught in airstreams, and drops fell into our world, forever illuminating the poetry of men. With this diversion, Odin bought a few moments to manoeuvre and he crossed safely into the realm of the Aesir.

Suttungr knew the chase had ended and flew back to brood upon revenge in his silent halls.

Odin regurgitated the blood of Kvasir and offered it to the gods, and to all humankind.

This lifeblood of Kvasir has since given the gods poetry. Some rare and select cups of mead were also given to humankind, and to the Moon-children, Hjuki and Bil.

EAGLE AND SERPENT

Psychological Integration

In the tale of the mead of poetry, we learn about Odin's underworld journey that stirs up soul-powers and breaks down barriers. Odin is looking for the waters of inspiration which offer the art of poetry. He shapeshifts into a serpent in order to release the wisdom waters (Kvasir's blood), which he will bring back as a gift of inspiration to the gods. As he travels into the mountain, he takes the shape of a serpent. The serpent depicted in many cultures carries the power to shed its skin, to transform and to unlock knowledge. In Genesis, the serpent reveals to Adam and Eve their own nakedness, sexuality – and with that revelation they lose their immortality, they become vulnerable. Yet, they gain the knowledge of what is good and evil.

The coiled serpent of kundalini rises up the body to reveal different states of consciousness and insight into the nature of reality, whilst it passes the many energy centers named chakras. The serpent can smell with its tongue, it can hear with its skin and is particularly sensitive to low-frequency vibrations and tremblings from inside the earth. Traditionally linked with secret, chthonic and oracular mysteries of knowledge, the snake is revealing an active penetrating energy of fertility and potency.

Also, the skin is shed from one initiatory passage to the other. The ouroboros, which is a symbol depicting a dragon/serpent eating its own tail, portrays eternity with the continual renewal of life. The tunnel Odin is drilling through is the pathway through to inner meaning, to be taken without getting stuck or lost. Much baggage, attachments and belongings must be shed, in this tunnel you can't bring your armour, weapons and shield; they won't fit in this narrow space. Once through the passage, there is a sudden meeting with joy, sensuality and beauty; the beauty the soul longs for after it has drilled through hardening stone, once our stone walls have been broken, the mask lifted. Here we find the beloved waiting for Odin in the depths of the halls. Across all northern mythic narrative, this is by going into the unknown, into the dark regions where the gods are given their powers, treasures and gifts. Our imagination is best served when entering the unknown, creative potential needs an undefined region to work within.

Once the return begins, Odin transforms into an eagle. He ascends into spirit and flies high into the world of the gods. When you merge the serpent with the eagle, a "winged serpent" is revealed – a dragon.

All across the world you can hear stories of this winged serpent: the Native American winged rattlesnakes, the Mesoamerican feathered serpent, the Egyptian winged-snake goddess Wadjet, and the serpent-tailed creator beings in Chinese myth. When a serpent is represented as winged, the eagle is present; forming a dynamic cosmic harmony of union between spirit and matter, heaven and earth. The serpent reveals the darkest times, the most difficult challenges (the raw tempering of soul) and the eagle flies high into illumination (the ascent of spirit). It's when these two images are joined – the serpent and the eagle – that we have the alchemical birth of the dragon. Here the dragon becomes a force of psychological integration and reveals a whole person who encompasses both hell and heaven.

The dragon speaks: you live a spiritual life, because you live a human life, that's enough.

Dragons are very rare in the world because they represent a complete psychological integration, a person with dragon wisdom can see his own shadow as well as light. In this way they do not project a shadow onto another person (or nation or group) – a prevalent attitude when the soul and spirit journey is not complete, nor integrated, but only focused on the eagle flight. When the Sun shines down on the eagle from above, the wide pinions cast shadows, the snake is alerted and slithers to its hidden nest. Similarly, when a person stands too close to the light, a shadow is also cast behind them that they cannot see, these shadows can become their projection, arrogance, pride, quick judgments and dogmatism. The shadow self (serpent) within lies hidden, unexplored, coiled and denied.

In the famous Greek myth, Icarus seeks spirit too soon and his uninitiated wings melt when approaching the burning spirit of the Sun. Where the serpent is banned or actively avoided, it gives rise to only a partially complete psyche. In the Mead of Poetry we hear how both the chthonic and the light are alchemically wed and that poetry and art is the soul-water that sustains an integrated psyche.

CHAPTER 5

Mother Holle and the Water of Life – Reimagining Ritual

"Rituals do what stories tell."

Micheal Meade

Over millennia humankind has developed two main vehicles to attend to the threads and mysteries of life through ceremony and ritual. What are the differences between ceremony and ritual?

Ceremony is something that is ongoing throughout the year and through our ceremonial practice we extend the lifeline of the culture where it is practiced. Even on Christmas Day, the famous and staunch atheist Richard Dawkins admits he sings in Church, where he is fully participating in perpetuating a particular "English" cultural landscape, he is helping to keep it alive.

The question therefore is not whether you believe in a god; instead, the questions arise: do you know the songs, foods, dances and the practices? Often we are blind to our own cultural ceremonial paraphernalia, not noticing how indigenous we ourselves look to those from other countries as we munch on our mince pies, sing in stone churches and gather at taverns.

We all partake in this process because when in ceremony we sense that we are part of something bigger than our own intellectual and emotional opinions.

A ritual, on the other hand, can be seen as an activity to change or alter an outcome, to mend your life's thread, to cast away something that is no longer serving us. We want to take responsibility for our own destiny. Such rituals are there to make a statement of intent. We gather in ritual for a purpose-driven activity.

Ritual is therefore the vehicle of magic.

We have a treasure chest of ritual stories all gathered by the Brothers Grimm. The old fairytales offer us profound ritualistic tools for a myriad of life events. Many echoes of the Brothers Grimm we can also see in the more epic myths of the Eddas.

RITUAL AS STORY: MOTHER HOLLE

Jacob and Wilhelm Grimm – 1812

A widow had two daughters, one was beautiful and industrious, the other ugly and lazy. She greatly favoured the ugly, lazy girl because she was her own daughter. The other one had to do all the work and be the Cinderella of the house.

Every day the poor girl had to sit by a well, next to the highway, and spin yarn so much that her fingers bled. Now it happened that one day the reel was completely bloody, so she dipped it in the well to wash it off, but it dropped out of her hand and fell in. She cried, ran to her stepmother, and told her of the mishap. She scolded her so sharply, and was so merciless that she said, "Since you have let the reel fall in, you must fetch it out again."

Then the girl went back to the well, and did not know what to do. Terrified, she jumped into the well to get the reel. She lost her senses and when she awoke and came to herself again, she was in a beautiful meadow where the Sun was shining, and there were many thousands of flowers. She walked across this meadow and came to an oven full of bread. The bread called out, "Oh, take me out. Take me out, or I'll burn. I've been thoroughly baked for a long time." So, she stepped up to it, and with a baker's peel took everything out, one loaf after the other.

After that she walked further and came to a tree laden with apples. "Shake me. Shake me. We apples are all ripe," cried the tree. So, she shook the tree until the apples fell as though it were raining apples. When none were left in the tree, she gathered them into a pile, and then continued on her way.

Finally, she came to a small house. An old woman was peering out from inside. She had very large teeth, which frightened the girl, and she wanted to run away. But the old woman called out to her, "Don't be afraid, dear child. Stay here with me, and if you do my housework in an orderly fashion, it will go well with you. Only you must take care to make my bed well and shake it diligently until the feathers fly, then it will snow in the world. I am Frau Holle."

Because the old woman spoke so kindly to her, the girl took heart, agreed and started in her service. The girl took care of everything to Frau Holle's satisfaction and always shook her featherbed vigorously until the feathers flew about like snowflakes. And, so, she had a good life with her, there were no angry words, but boiled or roasted meat every day.

Now after she had been with Frau Holle for a time, she became sad. At first she did not know what was the matter with her, but at last she determined that it was homesickness. Even though she was many thousands of times better off here than at home, still she had a yearning to return. Finally, she said to the old woman, "I have such a longing for home, and even though I am very well off here, I cannot stay longer. I must go up again to my own people."

Frau Holle said, "I am pleased that you long for your home again, and because you have served me so faithfully, I will take you back myself." With that, she took her by the hand and led her to a large gate.

The gate was opened, and while the girl was standing under it, an immense rain of gold fell, and all the gold stuck to her, so that she was completely covered with it. "This is yours because you have been so industrious," said Frau Holle, and at the same time, she gave her back the reel which had first fallen into the well.

With that, the gate was closed and the girl found herself above on earth, not far from her mother's house.

Then she went inside to her mother and, as she arrived all covered with gold, she was well received, both by her mother and her sister. The girl told all that had happened to her, and when the mother heard how she had come to the great wealth, she wanted to achieve the same fortune for the other ugly and lazy daughter. She made her go and sit by the well and spin. To make her reel bloody, the lazy girl pricked her fingers and shoved her hand into a thorn bush. Then she threw the reel into the well, and jumped in herself.

Like the other girl, she too came to the beautiful meadow and walked along the same path. When she came to the oven, the bread cried again, "Oh, take me out. Take me out, or else I'll burn. I've been thoroughly baked for a long time."

But the lazy girl answered, "As if I would want to get all dirty," and walked away.

Soon she came to the apple tree. It cried out, "Oh, shake me. Shake me. We apples are all ripe."

But she answered, "Oh yes, but one could fall on my head," and with that she walked on.

When she came to Frau Holle's house, she was not afraid, because she had already heard about her large teeth, and she immediately began to work for her. On the first day, she forced herself, was industrious and obeyed Frau Holle – she was thinking about all the gold that she would give her. But on the second day, she already began to be lazy. On the third day, even more so, and then she didn't even want to get up in the morning. She did not make the bed for Frau Holle the way she was supposed to, and she did not shake it until the feathers flew. Frau Holle soon became tired

69

of this and dismissed her of her duties. This was just what the lazy girl wanted, for she thought that she would now get the rain of gold.

Frau Holle led her too to the gate. She stood beneath it, but instead of gold, a large kettle full of black pitch spilled over her. "That is the reward for your services," said Frau Holle, and closed the gate.

Then the lazy girl went home, entirely covered with pitch.

The pitch stuck fast to her, and did not come off as long as she lived.

*Therefore, in Hessen whenever it snows, they say that Frau Holle is making her bed.

The Ritual

The Mother Holle story is transmitting cultural and ritual information on the maturing process of "girl to womanhood." For fairytales to survive in the general imagination for hundreds of years, they need to have a substance in them which provides an "anatomy of our psychology" (Marie Von Franz).

The relationship between mother and daughter is paramount in our society, as in the societies hundreds of years ago when the story was formed. Here the fairytale functions as a guide for the developmental process from childhood to adulthood. Our protagonist goes through symbolic steps which are passages of time and seasonal changes to reach maturity (it is by jumping into the WELL that the journey begins into a magical land where she is alchemically transformed).

The change of seasons and passages of time in the story can be seen in the following steps:

Spring – The wildflowers
Summer – The bread
Autumn – The apples
Winter – Shaking Mother Holle's bed covers and it snows

Mother Holle has been associated with the winter and the wild hunt in many parts of Europe where she controls the snowfall. The folklorist, Eugen Mogt, points out that Mother Holle is one of the leaders of the wild hunt alongside Odin.

"Like Wodan (Odin), she too rode through the air, most especially during the time when the souls of the dead were about, during the twelve nights. Throughout central Germany she appears at the head of the spectres from the underworld as Frau Holle, who tangles the yarn of lazy spinners and punishes them, rewards good children, punishes bad, and who lives in mountains and ponds or lakes like the dead."

In the beginning of the plot we are introduced to the spindle and the blood, which informs us that a "maturing" process is under way – the biological function of moving into womanhood. The place where women gathered to spin flax is related to the female mysteries, from the Mediterranean up to northern Europe. We hear about spinning in the "Briar Rose" and "Rumpelstiltskin" – all well-known stories, but there are others too such as: "The Tale About the Nasty Spinning of Wax," "The Spindle, the Shuttle, and the Needle," "The Lazy Spinner" and "The Three Spinners." It took a long time to spin flax or wool into yarn, 15 kilometers of yarn needed to be made in order to create 5 metres of fabric. The technique was to hold the distaff under one arm and wrap fiber around it, then pull out the fiber and then twist it into thread.

The thread was wrapped around a spindle. The practice of Seidr relates to spinning and weaving, the wyrd is often depicted as a spun carpet. Spells were cast and stories told whilst spinning. Because of this, it is not difficult to imagine that it was regarded rather unmanly to practice Seidr in the old times. The three bright stars of Orion's Belt are also called Frigga's Distaff, which indicates the idea of the goddess spinning the threads with the Moon, Sun and stars – all embroideries in her weaving.

> "A wife of noble character who can find? She is worth far more than rubies … In her hand she holds the distaff and grasps the spindle with her fingers."
>
> – Biblical Proverb.

The Well

Von Beit says this of the well:

> "The well, with its deep surface reminiscent of a watery mirror, is a frequently occurring symbol of the magical realm or land of souls. It is equipped with motherly qualities and distinctly associated with birth. A popular belief says that small children come from the well. In Germany, these are called Holle Wells where the stork gets her children."

The well is also a container, relating to the rune Petra ᚲ – a place where souls are born and made. The well is an initiatory portal, which we need to gaze into to find the wisdom we need to complete our individuation. The well connects us to the deep water in the earth that we have to dig to find. The well leads to the underground, the deep shafts that are part human and nature. Human hands create the well as they seek for the water below. We dig for the waters below and the wellsprings in ourselves are filled with our feelings, and deepest imagination. In our story, the well is a portal into another world – into the world of Mother

Holle, and there are instructions and work to be done in this world, to transform activities, feelings, work, virtues and ethics into alchemical gold.

The baking of bread, after the blood, points to pregnancy or a pregnant possibility – we have the old saying, "the bun in the oven."

Apple trees indicate life and especially maturing life, when they are ripe they are also revealing the autumn season here. Apples are related to the Goddess Idun who in Scandinavian mythology tends the apples that give the gods long lives. Both the apples and the bread give us echoes of regenerative qualities and the first daughter heeds their messages.

She meets with Mother Holle and serves her throughout the winter. She does so diligently and is given her gifts and her maturation is complete. She is showered in gold. We de-literate the gold and instead read gold as we "feel" the sensation of gold to be. Our language here is a vocabulary of the senses, non-literal, metaphorical and close to our own feelings.

Ritual Performance

Background: Mother Holle is represented here as an old goddess of the north, the subterranean Hella – Hel.

Statement of intent: finding beauty, love and empathy in the coming-of-age severance of mother and daughter.

Insight into transformation: finding gold in the darkness.

Preparations and tools: apples, bread, string and a bowl of water. A cloth (the trembling veil) between the worlds.

Put out two chairs – one for the mother and one for the daughter. Fill a bowl of water. As a ritual leader, learn the story in detail and explain the proceedings. Use the runes to appoint Hella, unless someone steps forward, do the same for the mother and daughter. Please note: this can also be ritualized between a real mother and daughter who want to heal rifts or difficulties.

The process:

First daughter

Daughter being stained by blood whilst spinning her life by a well (not real blood – use a red colour, or ochre to show this if necessary).

Facing the Mother.
Told to pick up the spindle in the well.
Falls into the underworld.
Find divine sustenance in bread.
Collects the apples.
Meets Hella.
Hella instructs (soul instructions hidden as chores).
She longs for her spiritual home.
Hella gives her gold for her time serving her.

Second daughter (acted by the same daughter)

Mother wanting the gold for her.
Pricking her with thorns trying to make her bleed.
The daughter must hold the string which her mother also holds in this world to signify control and not letting go.
She bleeds because her mother is forcing her.
Falls into the well.
Encounters Mother Holle.

Works little and does not serve with her heart.
She is covered in pitch.
Returns.

Sometimes it can be good to reverse this, and the second daughter goes first to meet Mother Holle.

After the final return, the suggested daughter is confronted by her mother who feels shame and who does not agree with her. Here the voice of the mother is that of control and shaming. The daughter has to now find her own voice and speak back. Finding a voice and communication between them is important here and for them to talk over real life difficulties, or the ritual can break – this needs to take the time it takes. The ritualist and the people around will have to express their own voices and nudge them along for reconciliation, but not intervene.

Once the ritualized speaking comes to an end, there should be a severance that is made with beauty, sensitivity and respect for each other. The cutting of the string represents this, it can be done ceremonially by Mother Holle or the ritual leader, ideally with a given ritual knife rather than scissors. The daughter is then released and gains her maturity into womanhood. A new umbilical cord is now formed, one which carries the deep love for the mother, but it allows for the daughter to go out and seek her independence and build her own life as an adult.

Fathers and other participants drumming and singing and expressing their emotions throughout the ritual. This can be especially powerful if there is a mother and daughter that have chosen to do this ritual for healing and reconciliation.

To make this ceremony as meaningful and tender as we can, please see the above as the bones of a ceremony and add your own interpretations and choreography.

We are using a story which has powerful symbols and meanings that relate to a ceremonial past. A story to heal one of the world's most important relationships: mothers and daughters.

Once the ritual is over, I would suggest a feast for the daughter and a recognition of the severing of the string, giving her gifts and warm words of praise. She should also be covered in gold with praise words, and given gifts for a new found maturity and position in the community. It can also mean transforming her dress sense, braiding her hair, crowning her at that moment and much more – it is for the ritual leader to decide, the props around the ceremony can be as simple or as elaborate as we wish them to be.

The aim is that art, spirit and relationships can flower and for these rituals and practices and to bring reconciliation to relationships and the wider community.

In our modern lives, we still create rituals of sorts at moments of development or maturation. Though, more often than not, modern rituals are centered on practicality and have been shorn of much of their symbolism. Let's take the parallel example of the mother parting from the daughter, at the first day of university or college education, perhaps this is the first time the daughter is living away from home. The bags are packed, tears are shed, and maybe presents given, but the rich symbolism of the Mother Holle ritual is somewhat lacking. We live, see, and breathe the world through symbols, and if our moments of development lack them – then we may omit certain aspects of that development from those moments. Seeding these ancient rituals through our lives allows us to soak up and absorb the lessons at each life stage in a more comprehensive and poetic manner.

We can appreciate, comprehend and revel in the transformations of life, and our souls can develop with grace rather than with a knee-jerk necessity.

THE WATER OF LIFE

The Return of the Mythic King

A long time ago a king was very unwell as he laid on his bed, his voice was raspy and he had difficulty in breathing. He had not very long to live and beside him were his three sons. They were incapable of helping him. All the hopes of medicine failed them.

In the palace gardens they sat near a fountain and wept.

As they were sitting there, an old man carrying a crooked walking stick walked towards them. There was an occasional "kraak!" from a nearby raven. He looked at the three boys and asked what the matter was. They told him about their sick father.

The old man responded and said: "There is one thing that can help your father regain his health and his joy and that is the water of life, but to find the water of life takes courage."

When the old man left, all three boys were thinking about what he had just said. The older brother in his heart thought that if he could find the water of life maybe then he could inherit the whole kingdom. He would be famous and he would be given much wealth. He decided to go and find the water of life and went up to his father and told him about his quest. His father said what all fathers tell their sons, he said it was much too dangerous to go to seek this water as many have tried but very few can ever find it or even return from such a quest. The older son pleaded until his father consented.

He saddled his horse, the drawbridge went down from the castle and away he galloped over valleys, mountains and forests. Then he arrived at an old bridge and there stood a dwarf who asked where he was going in such haste. The elder brother responded:

"That is none of your business, move away you little dwarf or I will ride you down!"

The dwarf heard those words and whispered runes and spells. The brother kept galloping across the land when suddenly the mountains themselves, although he could see them on the horizon at first, seemed to come closer and closer to him. Over time, they towered over him and he rode into a valley where could neither go backwards nor forwards, he could not even dismount his horse – he was imprisoned.

As the oldest brother never returned, the second brother thought to himself: "Maybe if I go I will inherit the kingdom, I will gain lots of wealth." He asked his father if he could try and find the water of life. After much pleading, again the father consented. His horse rode over the drawbridge and galloped over the nine lands, just as his oldest brother. He arrived at the bridge, where the dwarf asked again why he was in such haste. The second brother looked at the dwarf and said: "You little shrimp! It's none of your business where I'm going and what I'm doing." The second brother almost rode the dwarf down.

Again, the dwarf whispered curses to the second brother. As the second brother was riding along, the mountains closed in, and he too was trapped.

Time passed without any tidings of the two brothers. The third brother thought about his own journey and quietly in his heart he thought about how this quest could help his father to regain his health and to regain his joy of living. He pleaded to his father.

His horse slowly made its way across the land, looking for the water of life everywhere. He looked in the sky, under rocks, he swam, crawled and climbed. He asked in many villages where the water was, but nobody could help him. But still he persevered.

Finally, he also arrived face to face with the dwarf before the bridge: "Where are you going?" Asked the dwarf.

The third brother dismounted from his horse and bowed his head to the dwarf, "I am looking for the water of life to save my father from a terrible illness and if I don't find the water of life he may not survive, the kingdom may not survive – do you know where it is?"

The dwarf answered: "Yes, I do. The water of life is in a fountain within an enchanted castle to the east from here. The door to this castle is closed to the outside world, to open the doors you need this black wand," and the dwarf took out an iron rod to show him. "Strike the door three times for it to open, behind the door are two large lions, and for them you will need a special bread." he took out a warm banqueter from this inner coat pocket. "This one has been baked with lots of honey, the lions will love that. Now, go towards the lion's roar, do not turn back but continue onwards and when they see you, give them your bread and try to go between them. If you are lucky, they will eat the bread, but they won't eat you," said the dwarf.

He rode to the east and there in the distance stood the castle. The words of the dwarf were true, because soon enough he stood facing two large iron doors.

He knocked three times and the doors screamed from their hinges as they opened slowly. There were no guards to meet him. Then, just as he had taken a small step inside, a terrible loud roar was heard in the gloom in front of him – the lions had noticed him. But he kept going forward, he didn't turn back. He walked towards the roars.

The lions jumped at him to tear him to pieces, but he threw the golden bread up in the air and their fanged mouths devoured the bread as they hadn't eaten for a thousand years. He had been lucky. He had time to find an open door that led into great halls inside the castle. There were torches lit on the walls. He arrived at the main hall where there was a table which held ever-fresh dishes of food. Oil lamps were burning and there were goblets of the finest gold. Sitting around this long table were a dozen princes, all dressed up in royal garments with bejewelled swords and rings on all their fingers. Their eyes were wide open but none of them spoke and there was no clunking of cutlery or movement, they were all completely still as if stuck in a deep trance.

The only movement was the light that flickered from the walls. The youngest brother went to each prince and pulled the rings from their fingers, he also took more bread.

There was a sword hanging within reach on the wall and on its blade were runes of power – he took the sword and slid it through his waist sash. He left the banquet hall to have a better look around, to see if there was anyone awake in this castle. He came upon a door which had the colour of a dark sapphire. He opened the door.

Nothing could have prepared him for what he saw.

In front of him stood a woman with such beauty that his heart trembled from the sparkle of her soulful eyes. The light level in the room was between light and the dark. Mysterious lamps shone from the ceiling, making wavelets of shadows on the walls.

She was wide awake.

The young brother was trying to hold himself steady, his own kingdom in his heart had received a sovereign queen.

He took a deep breath and said, "I am here looking for the water of life; do you know where I can find it?"

"Beware," she said, "you can take the water of life, but there is one condition: you must take the water before the clock bell strikes twelve. If you don't, you will sleep for two thousand years, and the sun-wheel is pointing to quarter to twelve."

"I am the princess of this enchanted castle," she continued. "I can see my own heart in your eyes. In a year's time, on the same day, I will be here waiting for you to return, if you are willing."

He made a pledge to return in a year's time.

He had to hurry. As he went further down the halls, again he saw another door. He opened it and found a wonderful bed full of warm downs; there he laid and fell asleep.

He woke up from the memory of what the princess had told him about needing to leave before midday. He rushed towards the courtyard and towards the fountain, dipped his flask into the clear water and then charged as fast as he could towards the black door. When the bells started to ring in the towers, the black door was closing – he ran and managed to get out but as it closed behind him, he lost part of his heel. He now would limp for the rest of his life.

But he had found the water of life, he could save his father.

He travelled homewards and again he arrived at the same bridge where the dwarf met him.

The dwarf could see that the prince had been successful and he was happy for him.

The dwarf told him that the sword he now carried can conquer any army and his bread can feed all the kingdoms in the world.

"There is just one thing, have you seen my brothers, do you know where they are?" Asked the prince.

"Yes, I do, but they are false brothers, be careful, they do not wish you well," replied the dwarf.

"Please, tell me where they are, I want to see them again," the prince pleaded.

The dwarf whispered another spell, and the brothers were freed from their traps.

When they were reunited, the youngest brother told them about everything about his journey, about the sword and the princess he had met and how he could one day inherit a kingdom of his own.

Together, all three brothers travelled back home. But the journey was long. When they arrived in kingdoms that needed help, the youngest brother brought out his sword of victory and he helped all the kings that he encountered against their foes; he distributed the bread, which was always replenished to those in need of food. Then all three embarked on a great ship. That's where the two oldest brothers spoke amongst themselves: "Our youngest brother is going to get the entire kingdom and all the wealth and we will gain nothing! He has gone through all the pain, but we will take all the gain."

In the middle of the night, the two brothers stepped into the cabin of the youngest brother and poured the water of life into their flask and replaced it with seawater in the goblet.

As soon as they arrived safely in the harbour, the youngest brother ran to the bedside of his father and poured seawater into his mouth.

"What are you doing? Are you trying to kill him?!" Shouted the other brothers.

Then the two older brothers poured the water of life into his mouth and their father drank deep from the flask. It was not long before his eyes shone with health and he stood up with vitality in his body. The older brothers gained all the praises for what they had done.

A court was gathered and people demanded that the king put an end to his youngest son who had committed treason.

The king decided that the youngest brother would be executed in silence by the old huntsman.

The huntsman had known the young brother all his life and he felt remorse and guilt at having to carry out these orders.

He put an arrow to the bow and pulled the bowstring back, he felt a sense of injustice as he was about to release the string, so instead he shot the arrow right up into the sky. The youngest brother turned around and asked him: "What's the matter?" The huntsman told him everything; he told the youngest brother that his father had ordered him to do the killing.

The youngest brother looked at the old huntsman and said, "Why don't we do this – you take my royal garments and I take your simple cloth? You can go back to the castle, and I will live for the rest of my life out here alone in the forest." The huntsman agreed and the younger brother went to live alone in that great forest whilst his two older brothers feasted and took all the wealth and all the joy that the kingdom had to offer – they had gained all the glory.

During this time, he lived in the forest. Wagons filled with treasures and gifts arrived for the king. All these wagons were gifts from the young prince who had saved him.

When the king received this, he marveled at the amount of this wealth and asked himself, could it be that my youngest son is innocent?

Meanwhile, the princess had laid out a road paved with gold for her suitor to come to her door. To her guardsmen she gave strict instructions: "If my suitor comes up towards the castle and rides to the right of the golden road, then he's not the right one, turn him away. If another suitor rides to the left of the road, turn him away. If a suitor rides right through the middle of the golden pavement, the gates shall be open for him."

The first brother remembered the story about the princess in the kingdom. He took to his horse and he rode towards the castle. When he saw the castle in the distance, the golden road shone and all the wealth in the world was laid out for him. He could not stop thinking about the pavement. He did not want his horse to touch the gold and instead he put his horse to the right of the road. The guard yelled out: "You are not the right suitor, please turn away – the princess will not meet with you."

Then the same thing happened with the second brother, who also remembered what the youngest brother had said. He rode out towards the castle. When he saw the gold in front of him, he gasped and could not stop looking; all the wealth almost blinding him. He commanded his horse to stay on the left of the golden pavement. As he rode up to the gate, the guard yelled: "Please turn around; the princess will not have you through the gates."

The heart of the third brother had been beating every day with the memory of looking into those soul-seeing eyes. When the day arrived, exactly one year later, he took his slow horse, which was not that slow anymore, and rode towards the castle. His mind was flooded with the sheer possibility of seeing his beloved. He did not even look or see the gold that was laid out in front of him; all he could think about was getting to the princess.

He rode right through the middle of that golden pavement, all the way to the gate – the gates were flung open and he was received as a returning king.

As the wedding preparations were underway, large heralded flags were seen from a distance. There was his father, who was riding there to be one of the honoured guests. He had learnt about the injustice and had come for reconciliation.

A king and queen were wed.

What happened to the two older brothers?

They went out to sea and never returned.

Looking for Inspiration, Coming of Age

The water of life tale is an initiation story of entering the kingdom of soul and spirit. The story lays out an esoteric framework that we see in the fairytale tradition, and an initiatory pathway.

Central to this story is to save a king from dying – saving the kingdom. Note that the kingdom is not "out there" – it is the inner kingdom. To use a phrase from Marie Von Franz: "The fairytale is the anatomy of the soul." The dying king is a common motif in many fairytales which points to a kingdom in distress – something has to be rescued.

The king symbolizes a self that needs to resurrect and through finding waters of life, inspiration and health can return. Anyone who drinks from this water gains a sense of purpose – a strong feeling of inspiration and deep fulfillment. The water eases away all pain.

The story asks: can we find the water of life today? When do you set out to seek it?

When we throw ourselves into fresh exciting and creative projects, careers, work and inspire new ideas, we are drinking from this well. But once we find it, we must protect it from the big brothers, our arrogance and our haughtiness can bring us trouble.

For many, the loss of inspiration can come when we have to build an infrastructure around our muse – the musician becomes an accountant; the therapist a marketer; the teacher a champion of health and safety applications; the eco-warrior transforms into a fundraiser; an inspired cook becomes a spreadsheet manager.

Once we build these infrastructures to protect our original inspiration, what happens to the water of life? Has it been stolen from us? Are we happy to carry on working within the infrastructure that we have to create to keep our dreams alive?

There comes a time when you need to go and seek for the water of life again, when change comes knocking. A call to adventure. If we stay rigid, we risk turning into stone and sleeping forever in the enchanted castle. Old fairytales tell us that we have to seek the water of life when our viewpoints and perspectives no longer support or give us any meaning – when our inner sovereign has become ill.

To find the water of life, we have to make the journey towards the enchanted castle, the underworld and our inner emotional journey. Sorrow and grief are driving the story and this is the motivation for the younger brother. Only power and money motivate the older brothers. Their path becomes cursed and they only receive a short-term gain, but they cannot see their own soul in the end – the beloved, the anima, does not open the gates for them.

The third brother, he has to wander off the beaten track and follow new voices. Note how his grief is not denied, he feels deeply for his father and travels through the underworld with the right spirit of intent. He is humble before the underworld journey into the enchanted castle – this is recognized by the earth-gnome (dwarf, black elf). His brothers, on the other hand, are deeply stuck.

In an essay that Jung wrote titled, "The Phenomenology of Spirit in Fairytales," often the old man or dwarf is presented as the "spirit" in the story and the spirit character is the one that can bring gifts and talismans to continue the journey.

In the mythic world we are surrounded by the forces of chaos (giants, titans) and cosmos (the gods). What lies outside of the village or city, the large forests, steep cliffs, or oceans are in the domains of chaos. It is also where the water of life resides; it's only there where the mead can be found.

The Greek demi-god Herakles has to travel to the underworld, or to monstrous lands where he has to capture or kill a beast that stalks on the edges of the village. By killing the beasts that are surrounding the world (or village), the mythological hero makes *order out of chaos*. Thor faces the Midgard serpent out in the grey waves, far off in the horizon. The journey of the hero is to an edge world, he travels where nobody has dared to go, to places where death and darkness reside. He is on a quest fighting for survival, not only for himself, but for his people and community. Here is a distinction of what makes a "true" hero – a lesser hero fights for his own desires and wants (like the two older brothers), whilst the true hero fights for that which is larger than himself and the community that is being threatened by chaotic forces.

Today, as we are looking through our excessive consumption, pandemics, overpopulation, climate change and resource depletion, we can see that the kingdom is sick. A calling is being heard – we require another hero to emerge, someone who is willing to step aside from society again in order to find a new "Herculean club" to defend our modern age.

The pattern is this: the hero makes a move away from his home, away from the people he loves and decides to take on the quest. As the hero is willing to sacrifice himself for the cause, he is often sanctified and deified by the village. The independent, free man riding on his horse (the John Wayne mythos) still carries a strong mythic symbol in the US with a psychological impact that reverberates today in capitalist society, but this hero is the self-made man; he is not a community man. There is no banquet laid out for him at the end of his journey – the independent man rides into the sunset alone.

A homecoming hero results in the overthrowing of the old as he takes the seat of the king. The hero's quest ends, in mythological terms, with him becoming semi-divine or rising to the godhead. In the myths of Jesus Christ or Buddha, both reinstate a new civilization on their return from the dead or the enlightenment experience. One experience they all face is a great "call to action" – usually an impossible mission with impossible odds, which results in an arduous journey where they face their mortality and limitations, once they return, they bring new knowledge and a new symbol.

The origins of all these hero myths are enacted by the Sun every day, as it rises in the east after a long passage through the dark. The Sun returns to us a blessing and a gift each dawn. The sunrise is the expression of light conquering the dark. The Sun is our first hero. All heroes are solar in origin.

In the ancient world it was never a certainty that the Sun would return after the dark descended and in many cultures the Sun was always greeted with a gesture and ritual of thankfulness each morning. The story of the Sun's journey is a seasonal agricultural journey. The light returns and the plants grow again, but with each winter a new hero cycle begins – each era demands a new Herkules or a new young prince. They work in the world of the present but also evolve with the zodiacs of their time.

The homecoming of the hero can be just as difficult as the outward journey. The hero stands to face the old king and the old customs which have not yet recognized his newly-found wisdom. This return journey is re-enacted each time young men return from their own personal travails and initiations, when through their experiences they have "earned" their right to become adults and now they can be part of the adult world. We see this in the DIY youth initiations of sex, drugs and rock'n'roll.

When the return is antagonistic to the hero, he has to use his newly won wisdom to overcome the king or the people that stand in his way. Sadly, this homecoming can be destructive – we see this with the reintegration of soldiers that return from fighting; those who have had strong psychological or religious experiences which their society is openly hostile towards; or those who have experienced an attraction to the same sex which they can't openly share; and much more.

Looking at this from the mythic view, if the hero's return is antagonistic, the hero then becomes an outlaw, a pirate, someone who is cast out. He has received wisdom, he has completed his quest, but the "gifts" he received or found are not accepted by the village and he is not welcomed back into the community – instead his knowledge becomes a burden, his gifts are not wanted. When generations are too far apart, the parents may not recognize their children's initiations into adulthood and they will not see, nor behold the gifts they have attained. It will all be a blur of tattoos, noisy music and philosophies they don't understand. Here, the greatest danger lies when the parental adult declines to offer the feast of a homecoming and instead judges their teenager harshly. This can lead to an early depression and an overbearing dependency on their peers, who are not elders.

The myths insist on the importance of a homecoming and the importance of the wedding or a great feast where the family is invited. Most fairytales end in weddings as the hero, finally back from his adventures, meets his "bride" and is reunited with his village – now he is finally at home and he is whole again. The wedding ring on his finger closes the quest and binds him to his homeland, binds him to the life of the householder.

From the heroic adventures of Odysseus we are quickly subject to the hero's one key attribute: his "metis" (skill and craft). He succeeds in overcoming his obstacles through behaviours that correspond to a "trickster" figure. Trickster figures, such as Hermes, are morally ambiguous in their nature; they do not live by the courtly laws of Apollo or Zeus and often come in conflict with big questions of "moral virtue" (similar to what youth culture does today). For example, when Odysseus' life is in danger, rather than using his strength to overcome his enemies, which we see in the figure of Herakles, Odysseus has to use his wits. Through his travels (which is also a "mercurial" activity) he has to learn to navigate in a world which is not black and white. Instead, he navigates in the multi-coloured world, the metis world – and for this he has to be adaptable. He needs to improvise brilliantly in the spur of the moment. A prime example being when he hides his men in the cave of Polyphemus and outwits the monster by offering him wine and blinding him with an olive shaft when he is the most vulnerable – when he is asleep. This is not the open battle we would expect from a morally strong chivalric hero.

In the hero of Akhilles we have the opposite values. Here the world is less metis and more black and white – we see the passion of a young warrior with a strong sense of chivalric code from the warrior class. One interesting point: Akhilles is forced to wear women's clothing at the court of Lycomedes. In the Viking myths, for Thor to one day gain his mighty hammer, he too has to first dress up as a bride to one of the giants.

Odysseus returns to face the old world and, through cunning, succeeds – he is revealed as a "true" hero and transforms from soldier to the king of the land and, finally, meets his beloved Penelope. The beloved is never a "spear-bride", nor is she a possession.

A mythical hero is a regenerative force for the community – the Sun returning in the spring is a reflection and origin of this myth. When the Sun finally rises out of the darkness and the difficult journey through nighttime, his bride; the Earth, chooses to witness him and she responds, bringing new growth and fresh shoots.

CHAPTER 6

Practicing Blot – Reimagining Ritual

THE PAST AS CEREMONY

The Blot

Here is a big question: how do we bring ancient ceremonies into the present to benefit ourselves, our families, and our wider community?

A "blot" (blessing) is a spiritual ceremony that is pre-Christian in form and shape; we read about blots in many of the sagas. A building where the blot takes place is called a "Hov". Other names for sacred places are Hörgr, Vé, Lund and Haug. Lund is like the "sacred groves" of ancient Greece. Haug means "a barrow" and is directly linked to the chthonic powers, the elves and ancestors, living within the earthen element. Christian laws forbade blot rituals in barrows and grave locations. Therefore, we know that blots (and seidr) were practiced in those places – it's paradoxical and unintended, but the laws against the Heathen practices by Christian lawmakers are now important academic sources in understanding more of the old Heathen culture.

For the early Anglo-Saxons, the month of November was known as Blōt-mōnaþ (Blot-Month). This later Old English passage points out:

"The month is named in Latin, Novembris, and in our speech blot-month, because our forefathers, when they were Heathens, always made a blot this month, that is, that they took and devoted to their idols the cattle which they wished to offer."

And more here from Håkon the Good's Saga:

> "It was an old custom, that when there was to be sacrifice all the bóndis [freeholders] should come to the spot where the temple stood and bring with them all that they required while the festival of the sacrifice lasted. To this festival all the men brought ale with them; and all kinds of cattle, as well as horses, were slaughtered, and all the blood that came from them was called hlaut, and the vessels in which it was collected were called hlaut-vessels. Hlaut-staves were made, like sprinkling brushes, with which the whole of the altars and the temple walls, both outside and inside, were sprinkled over, and also the people were sprinkled with the blood; but the flesh was boiled into savoury meat for those present. The fire was in the middle of the floor of the temple, and over it hung the kettles, and the full goblets were handed across the fire; and he who made the feast, and was a chief, blessed the full goblets, and all the meat of the sacrifice. And first Odin's goblet was emptied for victory and power to his king; thereafter, Niord's and Freyja's goblets for peace and a

good season. Then it was the custom of many to empty the brage-goblet; and then the guests emptied a goblet to the memory of departed friends, called the remembrance goblet."

What is the intent and purpose behind a blot?

My view is that as a verb, "to do blot" is to "ceremonially" create a relational thread to the gods, goddesses, spirits, ancestors, elves, land-wights and other local powers in the area where we live. This act can balance some of the debt we owe to the larger world around us: to the fish, the cattle, the great horses, the deer, the Sun and the Moon, the soils, lakes, seas, rivers and mountain streams – all that which works for us in the background, but in our daily lives we forget about and take for granted – this is best illustrated by the daily rising of the Sun. In the blot we attempt to return to balance – ultimately with the great Tree of Life.

Here is a question following from this thinking: in today's world, what would be a suitable ceremonial debt repayment to the motherly cow – the very wet nurse of humanity? How can we even begin to feel the magnitude and weight of such a thing, how could we even start to rebalance her service? With which words or gestures of beauty can we say "thank you" to those beings that have kept us fed and clothed for millennia? I believe these were central questions for the nature-based communities in the past, and there a blot had a real purpose of making environmental boundaries visible and in serving a function of remembrance of what we take for granted. In short, what you received from the land, you also had to pay back – and the blot was a ritual currency for the land, local spirits and the gods and goddesses.

Emma Wilby, in her excellent and much recommended book, "Cunning Folk and Familiar Spirits – Shamanistic Visionary Traditions in Early Modern British Witchcraft and Magic," writes about offerings to the fairy before the reformation in the sixteenth century: "At night, housewives across the length and breadth of Britain would leave out bowls of water or milk and plates of bread and cake on the kitchen floor for the fairies. By day, out in the fields and the animal sheds, their husbands would tie up cords and bury bones and mutter charms in an effort to please these capricious spirits of the land."

The fairy faith is still active today and we still see more mainstream remnants of this during the main festivals of the year, such as giving porridge to the local spirit (Tomte) in Sweden, or the giving of cognac and mince pies to Santa Claus on Christmas Eve. This can be seen as "doing blots" by entering into a gift-giving relationship and sharing of our "spirit-currency".

But just like any relationship, a blot ceremony needs to have its own balance of giving and receiving. We are giving the gods/goddesses or local spirits some of our own beauty, abundance, skills and time. The blot can also be done to hold a sacred feast with the powers as we do with friends and family – we invite the larger life to the table and share with our humanity and gifts.

The currency here is in our gesture – how much effort and beauty we offer up. The value then is in the time you have set aside to create and make these gifts. A bead you have bought from a shop would be worth less than one you have made yourself. A small clay bead that you have worked through the fire taking time and patience has more value than a golden ring with a diamond on it that you have simply acquired. A diamond would also have a big Earth-debt in the way it was extracted. I am sure this doesn't have to be spelt out, anyone can see this: in the eyes of the larger life, goods that you easily acquired through an exchange of money have less ritual currency. Effort and sacrifice mean something in this world and the world of spirit. Internal development requires a certain discernment and detachment, we are giving up the outer layers of ourselves to crack through the cold and unfeeling stone walls within our heart and, like the snake, enter the treasure within.

The three points to a blot ceremony usually are: the hallowing of the gifts, sharing them together and then offering part of them as a libation to the gods/goddesses, or other entities – the spirits of hills, lakes, mountains, fields, trees and rivers.

The modern expression of a blot is created within today's reality – animal blood sacrifices are not used as they were in the past. When our ancestors lived as farmers, giving some part of the slaughtered animal to the gods/goddesses and land would have been second nature, it would be an act of thanks and a gesture of appreciation and respect for the gifts of the animal through the year.

A Native American teacher once told me how some hunters would carry one extra arrow in the quiver, an arrow made with the finest feathers, gems, stones and braided with beads. His arrow would then be shot into the earth as a gift once the deer was seen amongst the thicket. Just carrying such an arrow would likely make you into a more respectful and selective hunter.

A horn containing mead (or non-alcoholic when appropriate) is the traditional and common libation. Here, the mead is blessed by the god/goddesses or the local spirit and ancestors, then the mead is drunk amongst the participants and finally poured out and given as a libation. Often the mead is poured into a ceremonial bowl called a "hlautbowl".

When drinking the blessed mead, we enter the ceremonial time and here words become important. We are encouraged to express gratitude, grief or praise for what has been, and what is to come. To stand with a horn in hand, tear in eye and praise your loved ones is something holy – you are exposed and opened, your lower lip trembles whilst the words are pushed through with difficulty. Speaking through tears means speaking the truth, a much sacred task in ceremony. To speak truthfully and to feel joy and grief in a ritual is an indication that the ritual is alive and has a beating heart, it gives us a feeling that gods/goddesses and ancestors are present. Some of the amnesia is being lifted.

Each of us has our own gift and expression in these matters and it's best not to critique a person's voice during the ceremony. The more deeply personal the blot becomes, the more important it is to have a freedom of individual expression. There is a deep well of feelings within people and some feelings have been hidden or suppressed for a very long time, to keep the blot open is the responsibility of the blot-Godi, or ceremonial leader.

Speaking such words into the air and giving them a voice is a magical act.

Preparation & Performance

Clear the area, smudge with local herbs, or sweep with a broom. The broom is a great banishing aid that was used to clear out anything unwanted; hence the witches' use of broomsticks. Birch rice and an ash handle broom would be most suitable. Also, a swan feather, found in the wild, is excellent at clearance of an area through fanning the air. Swan feathers are also good for fanning a person's hamr (astral body). Don't just take my word for it, try it and see what happens. This is something you can do to every blot participant, fanning them with a swan feather – it's a good alternative to smudging with smoke, as smoke can be an irritant for some. But if you are using smudge, then I would recommend mugwort, juniper, pine and rosemary – all excellent.

Singing a "galdr" or "vardlokkur" is also effective as a clearance ritual, especially those with strong resonating vowels. Vardlokkur translates as "calling in the wardens." A vard (ward) can sometimes be viewed as an old ancestral memory that can enter the space when the vardlokkur are sung. Something that happens to most of us when we listen to a song on the radio which calls back a poignant memory. Also, this is the time to place statues of the gods and goddesses and to bless them, or by laying other sacred objects down, such as pictures or materials from your ancestors.

You can build a "harg" which is an altar made of stone (cairn). I personally prefer a cairn if natural stones are available, because everyone can help build it together and it can remain there after the ceremony and can become part of a regular blot practice.

A start signal is a good idea – you can sing, blow a horn or ring a bell. The sound or song indicates that the blot is starting. Then pour mead into the horn and bless the mead with all the inspirations, peace, good-will and powers that are being called or sung in. The mead transforms into the water of life, the elixir of all that is holy and good, that which gives inspiration. Drink some if it, find some words and pass the horn and allow it to go around all the participants. Each one must drink their equal share – the world's problems could be solved if we re-enacted this in real life. The blot can be a social catalyst where we consider the importance of fair-shares. If sharing a horn is inappropriate for hygienic reasons, then everyone has to carry their own cup/horn and the mead is to be poured into their horns before drinking (just to reiterate, as there can be people who do not wish to drink alcohol, a non-alcoholic drink is fine to use as well).

Then pour the rest of the mead onto the cairn as a libation and gift. The more the cairn is used for this purpose, the more of a sentience you may start to feel within the stones.

Next comes hallowing the area with the participants:

You can dedicate someone to hold torches out in the four directions, or someone to walk with a torch around the people gathered (the eldest in the group for example).

As the participants join the blot, call out for reconciliation, to leave conflict and past grievances behind as we are entering a sacred dream time, a ceremonial time. If one grievance is pertinent and present within the group or family, then this is the opportunity to lay it to rest once and for all. If forgiveness is appropriate and possible, then this can be the right time to forgive and be forgiven.

The Blots-Peace (Blots-fred) is an oath that during this time there will be no bad language or conflict between the participants when the blot is ongoing. An oath ring can be used for this purpose. Try and not begin the blot until reconciliation is established.

A prayer is often a praise to the properties of the power in question and we attempt to give the same properties to those around us. For example, Thor has the property of strength. A prayer can be called to offer strength with his name and then it's appropriate to follow on to say: we will use our own strength to help others, in this way the prayer becomes an exchange.

Also, the "calling in" is an invitation, not a command.

Once people have spoken and the libation given, close the circle in the same way as you started (a call/blast from the horn), declare the blot as finished and part as friends.

Afterwards you can have a "ceilidh/gille" which means to celebrate together and partake in some of the food that has been offered, make sure to share the meal with the gods by leaving some of the best pieces for them on the cairn or a plate on the headed table. You can also make the ceilidh/gille a part of the blot altogether.

A theatre performance, music or storytelling is also great to include.

Please view the above as the bare bones, add your own ideas and imaginations as you see fit and are appropriate to where you live.

The most important notion is the rune Gifu X = gifts, reciprocity and reconciliation.

The Year of the Wheel

This text below from the Wheel of the Year is partly translated from Forn Sed in Sweden, of which I am a member: *samfundetfornsed.se*

Julblot – Midvinter Blot

One of the main blots is midwinter solstice; the Sun has reached her lowest point. Afterwards, the Sun will be returning. The big power here is Odin's character as Julfather or the God Jul, and also the God Frey who blesses fertility and growth for the coming year, when the light returns. Also, a few weeks before the solstice, the Goddess Sol (Sunna) gives birth to a daughter and she resurrects the light. This happens every year. As the old Sun sinks into the west, her newborn daughter returns. For those who have been to Scandinavia, this is today widely celebrated and is similar to the Lucia tradition: girls and women walk around in the streets and woods with candle-tiaras and offer gifts to all the households.

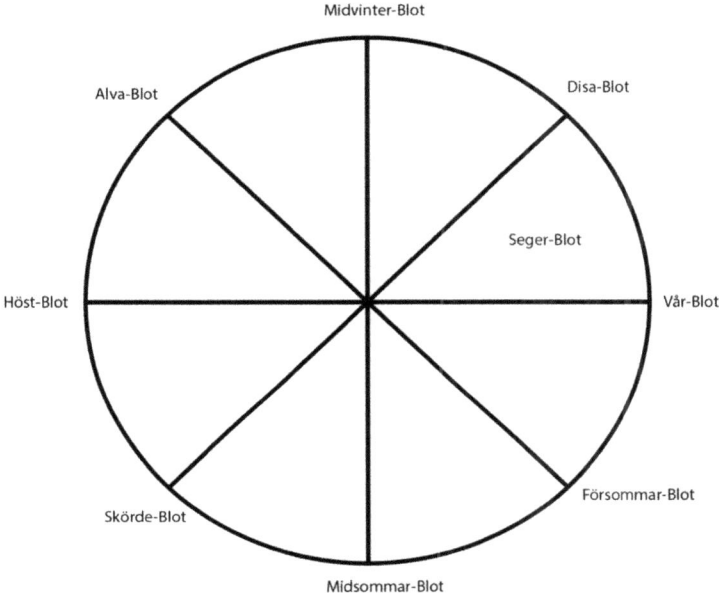

Disablot

Disablot is a celebration usually falling in February and this is for all the feminine goddess-powers. The celebration that the Sun has been re-born and the light is coming back to stir and awaken the seeds that are under the soils. This is the coldest time of the year and fire takes a central role in this blot ceremony.

Seger Blot

A victory blot for having come out of the winter! It can take place any day between the Disa Blot and Var Blot.

Vårblot (Spring Blot)

A time when the green starts to grow. This is a blot for the God and Goddess Frey and Freya, Sunna and the Light Elves. You can also turn to Frey's lover, the Giantess Gerd – her naming day is the 23rd of March.

Majblot

May blot – the summer is beginning and the trees are cloaked in green. This blot celebrates with lighting large fires, singing songs and also a walk in a procession with corn gods/goddesses. The "Corn Gods" bless the fields to strengthen their growth. The blessing is foremost to Frey, but also Freya, Gerd, Thor and Siv ochJord (Earth).

Here it is common in the old customs (Forn Sed) to create a ritual fight and re-enact the conflict between the spirit of winter and summer.

Midsommarblot

The Sun is at her highest. Dancing around the Maypole, eating pickled herring and the first of the summer's fresh potatoes. Also, beer and white grain alcohol is consumed (aquavit). This blot is dedicated to the union of Frey and Freya, in both their spiritual and physical union. The Light Elves and Sunna are also praised.

Sensommarblot

Harvest blot celebrated at the beginning of August – the summer is waning, and it's time to share the harvest. Much wheat is harvested: bread being central to the celebrations. Here the "Son of Jord (Earth)" – Thor is praised. Thor is the patron for the fields Tor and his wife Siv, whose hair is often described as a full-grown field – both oversee the fertility and growth of the farms.

Höstblot

Autumn Blot – thanking the summer for all the gifts! Time to prepare for the darker times again. Many practice Seidr at this time, and journeying. The gods and goddesses to invite are Sunna, Skade, Ull, Frey, Freya, Frigga or Odin. If you are harvesting, then it's appropriate to have a toast and speak words of praise for Thor and Siv.

Alvablot

The Elf-Blot is celebrated during the end of October/beginning of November. This is the big blot for the forefathers and foremothers – those who are no longer with us here in Middle Earth. The unborn are also praised.

This blot is dedicated to Frey, Freya, Odin and the elves. Frey is the King of the Elves. It is a time of remembrance. Some also call in the power of winter in the shape of the Ski Goddess, Skadi and the Winter God, Ull.

THE ANIMA LOCI

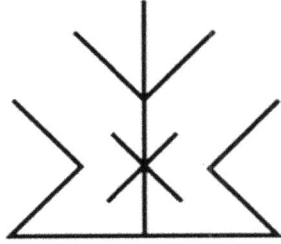

Building a Blot Relationship with the Anima Loci – Local Spirit

When we find ourselves in uncertain circumstances, such as we are living through today, our personas and relationships are revealed in higher definition. True friends (and enemies) reveal themselves in the toughest times. As much as a challenge, these times bring great spiritual opportunity, as magic and creativity is easier to unearth and work with, at least than in more static times. What is being revealed is often the difficult and neglected part of ourselves: our fears, our self-cherishing, or self-serving behavior. As Epictetus says:

"Circumstances don't make the man, they only reveal him to himself."

Any initiatory work worth its salt begins when we are ready to step up to serve something bigger than ourselves; be that serving a community, a river, a valley or a garden. Traditionally, the first being to turn to when times were hard in the homestead was the "Tomte" – his name in Scandinavia translates as "land" or "plot". Many children still see him easily. He is usually depicted wearing some kind of cap; he wears a red one in Scandinavia and is the embodiment of the animus loci (the local spirit). The different names and characters of local spirits are as varied as the landscape. In folklore we hear of brownie, elf, fairy, gnome, goblin, hobgoblin, imp, leprechaun, pixie, puck or sprite. Some aspects can be frightening, others benevolent and some cunning. If you are near the mountains and hills, the local spirit may be more giant-like; if you live by a well or river, it's probably more fairy; or if you are in the dark woods, then the associations will be more towards the goblins and trolls. The landscape often provides the character and mood of the spirit – echoing the voice and the personality of the landscape. The more elaborate the landscape, the more animated, complex and nuanced the spirit becomes.

The first step is learning to create a braid of relations between oneself and the local spirit. This relationship can be worked with whether you are in the city or in the countryside. If you do some research you will be surprised as to the number of stories of strange beings that reside in your area. The local spirit is a land wight who does not want the Earth to be abused; the spirit is a guardian of place and community often associated with growth of the land and its fertility. As what we eat comes from the land, this relationship is closely linked to our own health.

My first recommendation in this work is to locate a place near where you live which speaks to you deeply and there begin to give some of your gifts. The gifts can be words of praise, poems, letters, fruit you have grown, or anything else that you make by hand. What you create and give out becomes "spirit currency" between yourself and the otherworld. The idea is that within this currency lies the opportunity to make beauty within a broken world, to clear up a part of an area, however small, that has been neglected. To make it flower metaphorically and literally. The result of this practice is to transform emotions and alchemically turn them into gifts to the spirits of place. This relationship is a sacred undertaking and a life-long learning – it lies at the heart of the old Heathen custom. Progress in the outer world is reflected within the inner world.

This work begins and ends with keeping this relationship well-balanced and contributing to the health and happiness of the human and other-than-human community.

CHAPTER 7

The Labyrinth – Myth Cycle

THE RUNIC LABYRINTH AS A MAP OF SPIRIT AND OUR SOUL JOURNEY

Labyrinthine shapes of all sizes are found all over the world. When we come upon their pattern and symbolic expression in religion, folklore, dreams and mythology they speak of our life's journey and how it moved circuitously towards an unknown destination, a centre, a sacred space, a soul. The flow of energy is often depicted in the spiral shapes and the rhythmic notions of life, summer to winter, birth and death, the shapes move and can be glimpsed inside sea shells, within whirling galaxies, meandering rivers, highways, rail tracks, paths and landscapes.

The labyrinth journey is a key to understand our life's pathways, our suffering, bewilderment, confusion, darkness and grief, and also the wonderful joys with its music, kinship and great flights of spirit. The first thing a labyrinth journey reveals is that we must go through it, in order to come out on the other side. Unlike the maze, you cannot get lost in a labyrinth, but you have to keep walking step by step. Sometimes the labyrinth seems to go back on itself, other times you are thrown out from the centre – sometimes you get a sense of clarity, other times only confusion. The journey represents the commitment we have to our life's pathway and our journey to the centre. A place where both the soul and spirit can be united, where reconciliation can be forged and wisdom earned.

In stories we have labyrinthine structures, the protagonist moves ever towards her fate in the centre of the story. There is a longing to reach the "there" – to find something, some gift that can be used to help oneself or the greater community.

Stalking Soul

The Runes of Initiation

These pathways that we see in the myths and fairytales can be granted a wealth of runic associations. The stories can also be imagined and re-enacted as powerful ceremonies.

A journey in fairytale and myth always has two direct qualities: it is both chthonic and solar. The journey begins with the calling of the soul and the protagonist's troubled journey into the world of spirit. Once she finds the centre, then her life transforms into solar quality. The solar aspect is when we meet our beloved, have a moment of rapture, dance and sing and feel the great life current move through us with joy, ease and peace.

Here are some of the bones laid bare in this structure that we see in most fairytales and mythic narratives. I have used some imagery here from the stories that I have already written, but please add your own runic associations from the fairytales that are important to you. Here are some of the associations of the initiatory steps within the waters of life.

Serpent Path

ᚢ Ur – Beginning. The kingdom is unwell, the king is sick.

ᚦ Thurs – The call to action.

ᚨ Aiss – The process of transforming fear into trust. Taking advice from the dwarf.

ᚱ Reid – A sense of direction, a movement towards a goal, knowing the direction.

ᚲ Ken – Willpower.

ᚷ Gifu – The gifts from the dwarf, the sacred bread that feeds the lions. Offerings.

ᚹ Wunja – Crossing the bridge over the rivers of the underworld. Crossing the rivers of grief.

ᚺ Hagal – The enchanted castle, the realm of the underworld.

ᚾ Naud – Understanding the need and deep meaning of your goal.

ᛁ Iss – Stagnation, unmoving. Ice. Asleep. Thrown into chains.

ᛃ Jera – The thawing of the ice, new waters surging up, healing a possibility. The promise of a new year.

ᛈ Petra – The fountain which contains the water of life. The place where your gift and inspiration resides, transformation.

Eagle Flight

ᛇ Eihwaz – The young prince sharing his sword and bread with the other kingdoms, sharing his gifts. Using his talisman.

ᛉ Algiz – The animal intelligence that helps to navigate through the lands, in this case his horse.

〈 Sol – Riding over the golden road.

↑ Tyr – Sense of justice is restored in the kingdom.

ᛒ Bjarka – The meeting with the beloved.

ᛗ Ehwaz – Riding between the worlds, riding over the bridge which binds them.

ᛘ Mannaz – All that was given is now returned, the treasures being sent back to the king.

ᚱ Laguz – The waters of inspiration, the waters of life are flowing. Emotions are life-giving – healing waters.

◊ Ingwaz – Fertility, possibility and pregnancy.

ᛉ Odal – At the ancestors table, returning the gift to the community, feasting with family. The wedding.

ᛞ Dagaz – The final transformation from prince into a sovereign king, princess to queen.

ᚠ Fehu – A spiritual home, hearth fire.

If you add runic associations to fairytales in this way, you will gain an insight and the symbols themselves will become sentient and alive with meaning of what is happening to our lives today.

(For more information on the initiatory pathways of runes, please also see Thomas Karlsson's book, "Nightside of the Runes.")

Difference between Signs and Symbols

A runic "sign" becomes a letter to write with as it stands for a particular entity that is collectively known. Alphabets and languages are collections of signs; signs are objective, you cannot make them subjective, if you do, then the written language loses its purpose. A runic symbol, on the other hand, has a living meaning that will shift to fit its era and yet remain stable enough to encapsulate timeless human concepts. It is something to experience; this is the empowering part of the runic labyrinth.

Symbols attend to the artistry of our own aesthetic nature, they are sentient and can change our perspectives of ourselves and our behavior, especially when we use symbols as psychological and spiritual aids. More ancient written languages or glyphs tended to use more symbolism and pictorial form, our modern alphabet is hyper-functional and far more mechanistic. It's engineered to transfer tight and consistent meaning. The most common use for symbols and signs today is the branding of commercial entities and brands – and creating a mythological mimicry and symbolism behind that, we need to reclaim our symbols back into our spirit where they belong and where they can do more work than just shopping for goods and services.

An example:

A woman visited an ecopsychologist for her social anxiety disorder. She was unable to participate in groups and found it unbearable to be in coffee rooms with colleagues or, goodness forbid, after-work parties. Her counsellor told her to learn the "Mountain Lion Dance" in detail – this dance was going to help her to regain her power and her self-esteem.

When she had learnt the basic movements, she was told to go out into the wild and dance in full abandon, and to court the spirit and the power of the mountain lion through her dancing. This courting also happened in an area where the presence of the mountain lion was real.

She camped alone the first night in the forest and the next day prepared for the dance.

She started to move her body and limbs and re-enacted the mountain lion in the dance, roaring and jumping until in her mind she merged into the shape of the large wildcat. Then between the trees she beheld a mountain lion in its full living and sentient splendor. The mountain lion witnessed her and allowed her to be there in that realm. Through her dance she had been touched by the spirit of the mountain lion. Such a meeting can never be forgotten and she will carry the symbol of the mountain lion with her for the rest of her life. When she returned to her workplace, she was far more capable of overcoming her social anxieties and a new vital and wild energy had made itself known to her. This is an example of how a flowering of symbolic consciousness can overcome psychological barriers and strengthen the spirit.

Seeking our Soul

Meeting with our beloved is the moment when our soul can be glimpsed, when it is glimpsed in its fullness, in light and dark, in joy and pain.

These three stories I have collected and translated all share the desire to go out and seek the soul, to enter the labyrinth and there to catch a glimpse of the great love, or the true love – which is always the authentic love.

First is the desire for the journey, and then there is the reality of boundaries, which reveals itself as the journey into the dark parts of ourselves.

This is the hard work as we begin to open the gates to authentic love.

In all these stories there is a broken piece and a great wound that finally leads the protagonist to the destination of being united with his or her soul. This love flowers when the unknown is revealed and when limitation is recognized and accepted. The love, once imperfect, can flower into something that has longevity and trust. Accept your inner nature as it is, without the need for control, which often is directly weaponized as seduction and desire. In authentic love, both partners find equality and freedom. The old idea of the soul being male in a female and female in a male is exposed through all these rich metaphors in these stories. Sometimes we have many female and male souls in us.

In the poly-sensorial world of the soul, nothing can be trapped, all of it moves in the emotional waters of being a human being.

All three stories teach us that love is never the love for power.

CLASSICAL SOUL-BRIDE: THE UNDERWORLD JOURNEY OF ORPHEUS

A tree rose from the earth. O pure transcendence –
Orpheus sings: O tall oak in the ear!
All was still. And then within that silence
He made the sign, the change, and touched the lyre.

One by one they crept out from the wood,
emptying each set and form and lair;
and looking in their eyes, he understood
they'd fallen quiet in neither stealth nor fear

but in their listening.
Maria Rilke's "Sonnets of Orpheus" (1923).

The hard calluses on the hands of Orpheus were not formed by wielding the axe handle, pulling the reins of the oxen or from using a heavy scythe. Rather, they were shaped by the careful twisting of silver threads around the tuning pegs of his lyre, which he turned and pulled with great effort until the wood creaked and he was fully satisfied with the pitch, vibration and sound.

Tuning the lyre was an observance Orpheus made each day as Selene, Goddess of Moon, faded into the west.

When the first light of the Sun revealed the wilds of Greece, a high toppled wave of harmonious melody emerged from his strings. Birds swooped down from the heavens to sing alongside his music and the tamarisk, oak, chestnut, pine, cypress, carob and evergreen plane tree all heaved their roots out of the ground and began to fill the valleys with an old arcane tree dance, swaying with their woody and leafy limbs. Whales rose from the deep and their blowholes filled the air with mist and vapour as they swam close to the sea-shore to listen; all animals that see in the dark, swim, fly and crawl were drawn in from all directions to hear his music and, just for an instant during the dawn hour, all those that gathered heard the unity in all of creation.

When the music stopped, the trees sank their roots back into the ground as the whales sank below the waves, the birds and animals found their nests and burrows. The trees stopped where they were and configured standing tree-circles, from those circles were brought into existence the sacred groves of the ancient world – places where people carry their offerings and libations to the gods of Olympus.

Orpheus wandered all over ancient Greece and played his music. His wanderings took him high over the mountains of Rodopi and deep into the oak forests in the Peloponnese. A wheel inside of him was in constant motion, it was a wheel that turned in longing to be with his muse that so inspired his music, the one who had given him his art. He had never seen her; he had never met her face-to-face.

One morning as he sat by water born from the glaciers of the mountain range of Pindus, he could feel the presence of the river nymphs. There he called out for her.

"My mind is flooded with longing to see you, the source of my song!"

His voice trailed across the surface of the river. The water rippled as she answered him. She surged up to meet him from deep currents. She was water, she was river and he witnessed her for the first time.

Nothing could have prepared him for this meeting.

She was not the muse from the rose garden or the cultivated earth, she was from the wild murmuring, purling and cascading river, born of a deep current. His heart trembled when he beheld her soul-seeking eyes. At the moment of their meeting, Eros shot his love bow and emptied his quiver of arrows into both of their hearts. From that day she was forever the sovereign queen of his heart and he the sovereign king in hers. It was love with a scent of honeysuckle which drifted unhindered on a southern breeze up to Mount Olympus itself, there it loosened the silken tapestries of the gods and streamed into the wide bronze halls. A fragrance of joy infused Olympus; the gods were in awe as they gazed below and saw their affection, tenderness and yearning.

During the time of their first meeting, Orpheus and Eurydice were protected from the world as they laid together upon the wild thyme, free of care, free of sorrow. The music of the lyre poured out songs of such supernatural symphony and sensual elation that few, even amongst the gods, had ever known such pleasure under the broad-bladed leaves. The forests and glades were their delight and open meadows their resting place.

But the stars of the great zodiac moved and a new time approached. Orpheus and Eurydice left the wild to share their love with the people and community of Athens.

Next to the fountain sacred to the muses, Orpheus and Eurydice wedded. The high priest of the gods, Hymen, was called down from Mount Olympus to take the proceedings and oversee the ceremony. Musicians travelled from all directions to join the celebrations and people who drank from the fountain received blessed inspiration, happiness and long life. The wedding night was pregnant with the sound of music, cicadas, laughter; the satyrs of the woodlands led the dances and poured out the wine from the sunny vineyards of Dionysus. Animals and mankind celebrated their pledge of love side by side.

But as Hymen uttered his prayers during the ceremony, a dark smoke wafted from the incense bowl and stung his eyes.

There was something in the smoke that caught the back of his throat just at the time of pronouncing his last blessing. Once his throat cleared, he turned to his priests and whispered:

"A hungry spirit entered the temple, this is a bad omen."

Indeed it was.

The next morning, Eurydice decided to rise alone to greet Helios. She was joyful as she held in her heart all possibility for a future with Orpheus. Her movements were of delight, each step was a bright motion of feeling.

But in the grass something slithered towards her in rippling tremors.

Eurydice was unaware of the danger until the snake was within striking distance. It bit into her ankle and injected all the lethal poison that it contained within its body, then it vanished.

Her colour left her face, the fluid movement of her dance went stiff, she collapsed to the ground.

Orpheus found her lying in the grass as a broken-necked swan; he gathered her up in his arms and carried her limp and lifeless body back to his chamber. He tried to revive her with the healing arts as he invoked the Goddess of Cures. She heard his prayers but the eyes of Eurydice remained open and unanimated, her gown was wet and soaked from his tears.

He knew that it was too late. Eurydice's soul had fled her body.

When the news spread across Athens, the heralded flag of the king was brought down, horses were kept in their stables, markets were emptied, Piraeus' harbour with its large galleys was silent – people sunk into sorrow.

The only sound that could be heard was a lonely funeral drum which struck a terrible blow to summon the funeral procession. People hummed laments as Orpheus laid Eurydice's veiled body onto a bed of carnations. An ox-driven chariot was pulled through the streets. People walked alongside her body bringing oil lamps from their homes, forming a necklace of light that progressed all the way towards the Acropolis.

On the southeastern slope of the Acropolis, a pyre made of wood was prepared by the high priest. Orpheus placed Eurydice's body on top of the kindling. Two gold obol coins were laid down on her eyelids as payment for Cheron, the ferryman, to take her soul over the dark river. The double-headed bronze axe fell, and the white ox was felled, his warm blood flowing into the ground to the chthonic gods beneath.

When the sacrifice was over, the sacred meat was cut and shared amongst gods and people. The sound of mourning echoed in the Acropolis for a night and a day, until Hyman held up a torch high above his head and recited the funeral hymn and placed the keen flame amongst the kindling – the fire's hunger devoured Eurydice's body.

Orpheus bent his head as the flames engulfed his beloved, the fire burnt until only the white dust from her bones remained. When the dirges and the drum beat faded, a large pit of debris remained in the scorched heart of Orpheus. He took a step forward and touched the ashes of Eurydice; this act was an offence to the ruling house of Zeus and Hera. Then he grabbed a handful and raised his hand and poured the ashes over his face and reached down to the libation of ox blood and smeared it over his brow.

He turned to the mourners, raised his head up and made a covenant to the people of Athens:

"I will only return to this world, if I can bring Eurydice back. To do that, I will go and find the caves of Taenarum and challenge the King of Death in the world beyond light and beyond life. I pledge on Eurydice's white ashes that I will find a passageway into the land of the dead."

With those words, Orpheus walked out of Athens and went into the wild, the waters there were now cold and dark, emptied of the spirit of his muse. The cold stark light of day hurt his eyes and exposed his broken spirit; he longed only for night.

He wandered for many years, lost in grief. His days were spent tracking the scent of his beloved, with his hands into the soil, he looked for her spirit-tracks, each hour he seized at her memory.

Taenarum's cave is strictly forbidden for any mortal man to enter. Orpheus knew that only the spirits of shadow would know of its orientation. During auspicious moon cycles and using the thaumaturgical and magical arts, he lifted his left hand to his heart and, with his right index finger, inscribed circles, letters and names into the soil and uttered words of incantation to wraiths living beyond the light.

"Spirits of the world of shadow, I am Orpheus, I am looking for the old passage to the mouth of Taenarum's cave. Please grant me the wish to find it, please aid me!"

As the years passed, his prowess at tracking gained momentum and his dark arts waxed more elaborately. Until the powers answered him:

"For your request at finding the tracks of the dead leading to Taenarum, there is a high price to pay. Only your very own heart can be used as payment if you are willing to journey into the darkness of the world."

To this he responded:

"You can gorge yourselves at my heart, as long as you can leave some life in it to continue my journey, so that I can continue to remember the face of my beloved when I cross the dark river of forgetfulness."

They agreed to his price.

Invisible spirits pierced his breast and his chest was ripped open. When it was done, life was only thin inside Orpheus. The Goddess of Cures came to his aid. A medicine spell was made; he was able to continue on his journey. At night he read the star constellations and the movements of the zodiac and by the seven stars of the Corona Borealis he received the wisdom that was promised. His eyes received the skill to see the spirits and the faint visible tracks of the dead leading to the twilight world.

He tracked onwards. The faint ghost-tracks were all he could see now.

Until one day arrived when the yawning abyss of Taenarum stood before him.

In courtly manners, he crossed both his hands upon his breast and bowed his head to the nine guardians of the entrance: Anxiety, Agony, Disease, Death, Fear, Grief, Hunger, Old Age and Sleep.

He held his head down to each one whilst he spoke.

"Guardians of the caverns of the twilight world, where the souls of unrest live, my fate has been spun to be hunted by a great sorrow. I assure you this gift as payment if you let me pass: for each moon that waxes and wanes, a song will be made in the dark places to ease those smitten with sin, punishment and despair."

The guardians held firm and refused him entry and the Guardian of Fear held him back.

Then, for the first time since leaving Athens, he rolled his silver strings over the tuning pegs of his lyre and tightened them. The wood creaked and groaned under the pressure and when he was satisfied with the strings most delicate vibrations, he started to play.

He praised the heavens; he praised Apollo and all of the Gods of Olympus. There was no more discord in the air; all harmonies of the world were conceived through his music. The nine guards were subdued. He moved through each one of them unharmed until, finally, he walked into the caverns lost to the breath of life.

There he journeyed down and down. The passages went left and right, right and left. He arrived in the Valley of Avernus – the Valley of Death. There he wandered under overhanging crags and above chasmic pits. There was no wind, no birdsong, no sense of smell, only a silent brooding.

Invisible spirits whispered to him, "Do not carry your broken heart amidst the world of the dead."

"My only fear is forgetfulness." Orpheus responded.

Orpheus' first hindrance was an overgrown forest of giant sharp thorns, which stung and cut him and left him with opened wounds across his body. He managed to wrap himself in some of his clothing to stem the flowing of blood. Then he walked into an orchard where rotting fruits were filled with poison; there under the bony fingered branches of dead trees he wandered for days. Further down still he journeyed until he heard the sound of water and his parched lips bent down to drink, but it was not water to replenish his thirst – this water was made of salt. He was drinking the tears from the well spring of each eye of every living mortal. He waded through the tears, then a deep current dragged him under. The river of tears was the longest river in the underworld. He managed to swim to the other side.

A second river stopped him from proceeding further, the widest river flowing in the underworld – the river of blood from war. Blood washed over him and he struggled in the whirlpools. Finding a calm current, he clung to a rock.

The third river was the darkest and the deepest: the River Styx, the water all souls must pass.

There he sat and for the second time he played with all of music's persuasive keys and sang:

"My will is unbent when my tongue has a song,
Where light is lost, I sing.

When free, no prayer can tame love's flight,
In my loneliness I grasp the lyre,
And weave songs from life's kernels.

I step on the lifeless path and I sing,
Where dark blossoms grow around lonely nests."

His music floated over the river and reached Charon the ferryman, who pulled his old boat towards him. Orpheus did not have the gold necessary to get himself across – without gold as payment his fate would be to wander up and down the shore as a forgotten spirit. As the boat made a dull thump against the riverbank, Charon croaked:

"I do not know who you are, but your music so enchants my ears that I will waive the payment and carry you across the river, it will be free of charge as long as you play your music."

As he sat on the boat and played, he perceived ghostly semblances of eyes in the dark water, eyes of those who had finished with the service of life; unwedded girls looked at him from the depths of that water and many youths who had been put into the funeral pyre before their fathers. Through his music, they found a glimpse of rest.

He sang until Ixion's Wheel stood still, until the Furies wept real tears; Tantalus forgot his fleeting pool of thirst, the vultures halted the pecking of Tityos' liver; and Sisyphus sat on his boulder, listening. The three-headed dog Cerberus with his coat of adders slept peacefully.

He traversed the river and arrived on the other side as a mortal living soul into the land of the dead. There all the drifting ghosts gathered around him, and he continued to play for them whilst he made his way towards the citadel of the King of Death.

Orpheus sank into faltering footsteps before he entered the lofty halls of the subterranean Zeus.

Inside those halls, time had lost its purpose. At the far side there were two thrones; in that domain a starlight was found in the dark. Persephone was positioned next to the Shadow, giving hope to the many guests of the underworld. Only the dark eyes of the old king were seen, his body indeterminate.

The light of Persephone was strong and within Hades was the ending of light – both light and darkness were wed to each other.

Orpheus faced them as a living man:

> *"Fate has led me hither to this hall of infinite silence,*
> *Please show pity for my forsaken and barren heart.*
> *I have faced shadows no mortal should bear,*
> *I have walked across mountains without stars,*
> *For the earth, the sky and the waters.*
> *Allow Eurydice, my love, to once more be unmade from this cold*
>   *abyss,*
> *For our love rouses the rivers, seas and lakes.*
> *In my anguish I have learnt of love's true mystery,*
> *That darkness is the mother of light.*
> *Therefore, I beg you please to awaken my love into light once more,*
> *To allow mortal love to survive the passing of time,*
> *And for I to take Eurydice back to the land of the living heart."*

His melodic incantation was heard and received.

Persephone responded:

> "The arrows of Eros have flown true and straight into you Orpheus and, as prophesied, love has carried you to our threshold."

The Shadow spoke:

> "You have shown me allegiance, possessing perfection in the arts and traversing obstacles worthy of Herakles himself. Indeed, as darkness takes away, it also brings forth. The third sister of the fates will find the thread of Eurydice's life to mend, but she will do it only on one condition: as Eurydice returns with you back through the Vale of Avernus, you must never turn your head and look upon her and you must be silent, or else this concession will be broken and it will fail. You must only look upon her once the Sun has risen in the east and shines upon your brow."

Orpheus stood with his head bowed before the King of the Underworld; there was a silence in the hall. He bade his courtly farewell.

Carefully, he walked away backwards and only when outside of the halls did he turn his back to the throne and walk from whence he came. He did not turn back, and he did not look back. He stepped into Charon's boat, but he did not turn back. Even when he could feel the breath of Eurydice on his neck, he did not turn back.

Having his beloved behind him, the thought of hope flooded his mind. They both waded and swam through the rivers of tears and blood, their love and steadfastness were their strength and their determination. They walked through the orchard of the rotting fruit. Orpheus could hear her limping as she still carried a wound from the sting of the serpent. They crossed the crags and precipices of the Valley of Avernus, Orpheus always walking in front and Eurydice walking behind. He did not turn back; they did not speak.

They journeyed through the valley and they entered the dark passages that led them back to the world of the living. The funereal tunnels took them left and right, until they could see in front of them the silver stars of the night.

As they walked out of the cave, they arrived before dawn with the air full of the dropping dews. Orpheus took a deep breath, inhaling the night air and as he did, he heard Eurydice behind him as she tripped over a stone. By instinct and care for his beloved, he turned his head.

There she was – a pearl under the stars. She stretched her hands out and his scarred and wounded hands responded. She touched his face.

"Is it really you?" She whispered.

They embraced.

But he had turned too early. He felt her body disintegrating as he embraced only air. He looked up and only a faint word of "farewell" echoed around him as Eurydice sank back into darkness.

He stood and shivered in a swoon, slain by both the bliss of seeing his beloved and the distress of embracing her emptiness. The nine guardians of the cave mouth approached as the perfume of Eurydice still lingered in the air:

"No!" He cried to them, "No!" He wanted to cast his soul from his body and follow her down.

He entered the cave mouth for a second time.

Back down into the Valley of Avernus, he followed her shadow and walked through the rotting orchards grasping at shadows. His body was frail, the cuts were open, his hair hung lifeless over his face. He swam through the waters and he faced the dark ebony River Styx. Charon did not hear his call; his lyre was out of tune. The only music that could be heard was the barking of bloodthirsty Cerberus from the other side.

For seven months he sat under an overhanging crag of the Valley of Avernus, his sustenance was the suckling of shadows. There he sang with the plaintive wail of a nightingale; a nightingale that had lost her featherless chicks from her nest. Since this time, nightingales always sing before dawn, in mourning and in honour of Orpheus, the twice bereaved.

When he stepped out of the cave of Taenarum, he was unrecognizable. His eyes saw the sorrow of all living souls.

He wandered to the windswept Haemus hills, where he built a simple house of stone. Inside the stone house, he crafted a temple dedicated to the God Apollo.

There, during each sunrise, he would play to the memory of Eurydice.

Women who heard his music started to follow the sound. In each song there was love and grief which they felt belonged to them. From all over Greece and beyond, women started to travel towards his music. Before long they stood and witnessed him playing under the stars. All fell in love with Orpheus as they believed that he played directly to their own hearts.

But Orpheus turned them all away.

As time passed, he was surrounded by women whose longing for Orpheus overwhelmed them. He sang to their own river, to their deep soul current; they all longed for such divine love. In his music was the memory of those flowery glades where once he had laid with Eurydice. Each note was a shimmering bell each morning.

The followers of Dionysus, the Maenads, heard this music and fell into a trance – their desire for Orpheus and for his love was unstoppable. They climbed up the hills to listen. Each one wanted his kisses and his affection. Bloodthirsty fighting began amongst them, trance turned into obsession, their eyes turned hostile as they looked upon him. Why was he courting an unseen spirit and not I?

They screamed for his attention and started to throw rocks and mud towards him. His music protected him from the stones as the harmonies provided an invisible barrier. The anger mounted, the screaming grew louder until his music no longer could be heard and then it failed to protect him. The Maenads took tools from a nearby farm and armed with scythes and spades attacked Orpheus with a force that was infused by their sentiment of being rejected and abandoned by love. Their power was such that they tore his body to pieces.

They cast his head and lyre into the River of Hebrus.

The head and lyre floated down the river towards the Aegean Sea.

The waters washed over the brow of Orpheus' head and rejuvenated him, his eyes opened and he started to sing. As the head sang, the leaves from the trees dropped, the rivers swelled and flooded the valleys.

The head and the lyre floated out to the Aegean Sea and ended up reaching the blessed Island of Lesbos. People who live on the Island of Lesbos have since always welcomed guests blown in from the difficult tide of the times. They took his head and set it high onto an altar, where it spoke to them of prophetic hymns of the gods and instructed the people in poetry, arts and mystery schools.

But on the eve of midsummer, the soul of Orpheus passed on.

The people buried his head in Antissa, on Lesbos, where to this day the nightingales can be heard to warble the same notes as from the lyre of their master.

As for the remains of Orpheus on the Haemus hillside, the Muses, all nine of them: Calliope, Clio, Euterpe, Thalia, Melpomene, Terpsichore, Erato, Polyhymnia and Urania collected his bones and built a lonely cairn, where they laid the gold obol pieces on his behalf and planted violets amongst the stones.

As for the lyre of Orpheus, Apollo himself took the shape of a mortal man and visited the Island of Lesbos to recover it. He strung the remaining threads to the highest musical pitch and cast it into the night sky and created the constellation of the Lyre, for all mortals to behold in the night sky, next to the constellation of Cygnus the Swan.

The God Dionysus punished the Maenads for their wrath and crime; their bodies grew bark, their legs roots and their arms tree boughs – in a state of timeless terror they remain today, lashed by cruel winds.

The spirit of Orpheus took the long journey for a third time and met Charon the ferryman. The muses had paid for this passage.

This time, as he crossed the river, he could no longer sing to those in distress, now he himself finally forgot everything; his fear had come true – he forgot his grief, he forgot his music, he forgot Eurydice. He became part of the drifting ghosts of the dead and he floated through a twilight world where time was lost to its own purpose.

Persephone witnessed this from her throne. His heart had been abandoned by the gods to a cruel destiny. She had heard his mortal song; she cried tears for the high price mortals pay for love.

Persephone collected all the memories for Orpheus. When she returned to Hades, she touched Orpheus' brow. She went to Eurydice and whispered all the memories to her brow and she too regained her memory of Orpheus.

Since this time, Persephone gathers all memories from lovers who have been separated by cruel fates.

Orpheus and Eurydice gazed upon each other.

In his hunger and in his thirst, Orpheus never gave up and when his love was only a shadow in his arms, he was the miracle who loved.

Orpheus and Eurydice walk together in the white isles, where immortal birds forever sing their praises.

NORTHERN SOUL-BRIDE: THE CURIOUS TROLL AND THE BRIGHT SUNBEAM

Original in Swedish by Hjalmar Bergman (1925) – Translated and Adapted by Andreas Kornevall

Trolls are wealth-suckers, they steal mountains. They are born from an ancient light, a moonchild of Earth, rich they are beyond the human capacity of wonder. A troll receives his long life through the light of the Moon and is shy of the Sun's light-daggers, as trolls see how quickly these knives cut the years of humankind.

Their appearance would be repellent to you in its grandeur. Their hair sits platted and dyed with saffron and inlaid with golden luxuriant threads. The tunic they wear carries beryls and black diamonds, whilst buckskin covers their shoulders in glinting amber and gold.

When moonlight breaks through the small holes in the granite rocks of their homes, they reveal deep chambers in the mountain. Pillars hold up lofty-vaulted roofs, painted and carved with contours and colours of linden leaves; a shine of deep-sea green spirals spinning towards the high vault; there to portray wildflowers and lightning streaks, underlaid complete with the mother-of-pearl. Every cloth hanging on the walls is woven from the jewel dust of corals, garnets, rubies and topaz. Each strand tells old stories of stone, axe and metal many ages past. Scattered around their studies are sculptures of the finest minerals, many are dragon heads carved and hewn. The carving of their fanged mouths is made of such troll artistry that you'll hear it roar the moment your eyes dwell on it.

Know that their treasure is unfathomable. Take heed, for those greedy souls who seek their riches, the paths that lead to their hiding places have laid silent and unstirred for any mortal foot to seek out. A troll can be bartered with, but never trusted – just like you cannot trust a mountain top, a hurricane or a naked sea-wave. Trolls and humans do not share morality.

But I will tell you this secret: those who are born from the ages of giants are now slowly starting to wake from a long sleep; they are waking from the forest, the forest you once called home.

Stories come to us from that twilight forest and this one is about how trolls fall in love.

The troll child's bed was adorned in the form of a hollow tree stump and the duvet was stuffed with the finest down. With all this wonder around him, the little troll was still not happy. He laid there and turned and twisted and whined. "What does this mean? Will he never get any of his teeth? Why does he not sleep? By the beard of the Troll King! It's broad daylight." Father troll would say.

A good and healthy troll child should only play during the night and sleep by day; for the rest of the time, he should not even murmur. His mother would call a human maid and she would come from a nearby farm to sing songs, but only in all the minor keys, as major keys are intolerable to troll ears. As she sang the troll songs, he would listen to the dark tones of the music and it filled him with delight. After a while, poor Sunna would start to whimper because the minor keys of troll music were full of melancholy.

When she had left, the little troll thought to himself: "In the whole world there is not one troll who cares about me." He pressed his hands to his stomach and began to cry. Only his mother could endure the sound. There is only one thing that can be worse than a troll baby crying and that is a troll father snoring and the house shook to both sounds. Whilst the troll house was quaking from crying and snoring, something happened: a silent large black cloud floated above the treetops with bright sunlight behind it; a sunbeam burst free and flew like an arrow towards the earth. Sun arrows germinate seeds, others can persuade a hesitant flower to bud, a third can sneak heat into an old man's blood. But not one of them is ever ordered to look into a troll's home.

It was by pure chance and partly because there was a tiny hole in one of the mossy tiles, and also because sunbeams are irrepressibly curious that a small sunbeam peaked through the split and looked around and discovered the little troll as he lay there in his bed. Her light almost went out; such was her fright at seeing the troll. She had never seen a creature as ugly as a troll before.

The eyes of the little troll opened wide. Never had he dreamed of anything as beautiful as a sunbeam.

"Hello you little troll. I must have accidentally entered your house. But I do not want to disturb you; you belong to the moonlight world, not the Sun. I must be gone."

When she wanted to leave, he cried. The sunbeam, who had a warm heart, stroked his cheek and said: "Do you not sleep during the day?" He rolled around in despair whilst down feathers started to whirl around the room. With the feathers flying everywhere, the sunbeam started to play with the delirious blanket and then she danced with the down feathers and ran the length and breadth of the whole dark nursery. Everything she touched got colour, life and movement: the green roof was in motion as if it consisted of leaves and twigs, the cobwebs glistened as clear as dewdrops and flowers opened from their dark soiled chalices.

The dust grains shone with the light of stars and created a small spiral galaxy that floated and moved in slow circles.

The troll did not even dare to blink for fear that the spectacle would end.

The more he looked, the happier was his heart. His troll tail waved when he tried to catch the sunbeam with his paws. He understood that he could catch it with his eyes but not with his paws. He thought to himself: "There is light in the world, whoever can catch a sunbeam will never know sorrow." As he laid there looking at her, she replied: "If you want to catch me you need to look for me." She managed to creep into his parents' bedroom to tickle his mother on her nose. Up she flew and sneezed and sneezed. She beheld the sunbeam: "A sunbeam, a sunbeam in our house! Wake up, father! A sunbeam! Kill her, kill her!" Swiftly and decisively the troll father grabbed a hammer and a plug, rushed into the nursery and thrashed his arms and fists around, but to no avail. Then he spotted the tiny, small hole in the ceiling and bang!

Sunbeam was gone.

Exhausted by sheer terror the troll mother held the little troll tenderly and wailed: "My beloved toad! My sweet snake! My sweet bat! What has happened to your mind? So, so terrible...a sunbeam in the nursery! Have you been scarred for life?"

There was nothing wrong with his health, nor did he become sick.

As an adolescent troll he grew up and learnt his father's ways to conjure and work with the old magic. In the twilight forest he built a large magic house which had a mill that transformed all

THE LABYRINTH – MYTH CYCLE

the dead leaves, grasses and flowers into black, fat and fertile soils. When he turned two hundred years of age, he was already a wealthy troll and when he reached five hundred, he was extremely wealthy and at six hundred, he turned into a mature and solitary troll, living amongst his hills with his gold.

But every day of his life he had thought of the sunbeam. One day, he decided to visit the wisest troll in the forest. His reputation was well deserved because for two thousand years he had never provided wrong counsel.

"I will give you a tenth of my wealth, if you tell me one thing: where can I buy one sunbeam?"

"Go to the old man on the Moon! He is a retailer of sunbeams and has large inventories."

He gave the wise troll a tenth of his wealth.

To get to the Moon, he took a hazel shaft and attached it to a long line and at the other end of it he placed a bronze sickle.

He hurled the sickle and it flew into dark space and took hold right between the old man's feet, who shouted to help him along, "Troll! Heave and pull, heave and pull!"

How he pulled and pulled! It took one hundred years, until he finally set his foot on the Moon.

The old man said to him: "If you are looking for a sunbeam, then you've come to the right place."

"You will receive two tenths of my wealth," the troll said, "for one sunbeam." The old man took the bag, which was full of gold,

"Look around and choose at will! Take a dozen and you will get thirteen with the bargain, I am not fussy," he said.

There was a large gap in the moon-mountains. It welled up a flood of shining beams. When the troll looked at them, he realized that they were not sunbeams. "Where I come from, we call these moonbeams." The old man replied, "Sunbeams they are, but I have taken the sting off them to make them bearable for trolls."

The troll was not satisfied, he took to his sickle and cast it towards his home; he flew like a large black bird through space, followed by millions of moonbeams.

It took him another one hundred years again until he could stand back on Earth.

When other trolls saw him return to their forest they crawled out of their holes and stumps and asked how he was faring. He shouted: "Much of my wealth I have offered and yet I have not met with one single sunbeam. I will give all my wealth to anyone who can help me!"

They shook their large heads. They told him to leave the moonlit forests. For, in the dark, he would never find the sunbeam he was looking for. They chased him out of the woods and he ran out of his world and found himself in the middle of a human village. Thankfully, it was night and all the doors and windows were closed.

All except one.

In the room inside one house sat a man next to a burning lamp, reading a book. All kinds of books were weighing down on his table and piled on chairs and sofas, books lined the walls from floor to ceiling. The troll thought to himself: "With all his knowledge, maybe he can offer one sunbeam to a poor old troll?"

He took courage and jumped into the room and ended up on all fours in the middle of the pile of books. The scholar was brave, "Science has long ago proved that there are no trolls in this world, but there you are in the middle of my living room. What do you want from me?"

"I am a poor troll who has given away all my wealth for one sunbeam. When I was little, I saw one and I have hidden my desire in my heart since, can you please help me?"

"Your wish can easily be met. Sleep for only an hour or two and when you wake you can choose between billions of sunbeams."

The scholar took a thick blanket and spread it over him; the troll closed his eyes and went to sleep. When the Sun rose up and shone straight in through the window, the scholar woke and whispered to the troll: "Look up now and tell me what you see."

As he lifted the blanket from his head and opened his eyes wide in the human world, a violent pain shot into his eyes, he saw for an instant the glow of thousands and thousands of lightning bolts.

"I don't understand, why is it so dark? Now I cannot even see the Moon, nor the stars, not even my paws in front of me!"

The man then attempted to bind him. He thought he would finally earn his fame as the one who had caught a troll, but the curious troll jumped straight into a busy avenue. Then commotion sounded all around him, there were old women and children, men and women and their dogs. Through only his senses, he hurried across fields and forests all day until he reached the edge of the twilight forest.

At first, the other trolls refused him to enter as he smelt of the human world. But when they discovered that he was blind, they let him stay.

A sunbeam was all that he had wanted and see what happened? Now his eyes were just two empty deep wells.

He sighed and sobbed at his predicament.

Sitting on a branch nearby, an owl hooted:

"Sigh not so heavily upon your own sorrows and sob not so wildly of your own pain."

The next sunrise, he woke by the sounds of faint crying, not from himself but from a woman; a human woman, she cried and cried because wolves were chasing her down the path. Even though he had lost his eyesight, he managed to run up to her and lift her and protect her in his arms. But the woman kicked and punched, scratched his face and pulled his woolly hair. He tried to speak with a voice as soft and gentle as possible. But she screamed: "You do not fool me, ugly troll!" She thought she knew about the nature of trolls, and she kicked and clawed. The wolves were ready to pounce on both of them. As long as he held her in his arms, she was safe, and he didn't let her go.

The wolves grew tired and stopped their challenge, the baying and snarling of the wolves faded and now they both sat by an old pine tree together.

"Tell me your name?" He asked her. She answered, "They call me Sunbeam, if you want to know."

Then he knew he had found what he had been looking for and had waited patiently for for hundreds of years. He lifted her on a pine branch high above the ground, he wanted her to be able to see the dawn and she did, it was like nothing she had ever seen before. He guarded the tree from any dangers as he would guard his own life. He was fulfilled.

The next morning, Sunbeam climbed down the tree and laid down in his arms. From that night onwards, she never left his side and fate gave them many good long years in the woven troll forests.

Human years are but brief, as they are ruled by the Sun; whilst trolls live for thousands of years.

One day, Sunbeam passed away just as she had left him when his father had filled the small crack on the wall. How easy and pretty had she played with the down feathers and dust and how she dazzled and lit up his home.

As he wanders in the forest, heavy with troll-gold, he often listens to the humming trees overhead and, at times, when the clouds break, a sunbeam comes and caresses his old face.

And for an instant he sees the entire Sun.

NORSE SOUL-BRIDE: THE STORY OF SVIPDAG AND MENGLAD

The Lay of Svipdagr (Fjölsvinnsmál, 17th century manuscript) – Translated by Andreas Kornevall

Svipdag was playing with a ball; it bounced through the courtyard, in through a door and landed in his stepmother's chambers. Embarrassed by the coincidence, he tried to sneak inside to fetch it. But before he left the chamber, she cast a spell on him, saying: "Don't you dare throw your ball at me! There is a woman called Menglad and she lives on a high mountain in a foreign land, she is longing for you. You will never rest until you have liberated her from her longing."

Svipdag went away knowing what he must do; he saddled his horse and entered his quest. Svipdag had set out to travel to the shores of the dead and his horse's hooves drummed across the landscape in ceaseless rhythm.

At dawn, he stopped before a large grave mound and pierced the silent brooding with his voice.

"Wake up now, Groa! Wake up, my beloved mother! I raise your ward-memory at the doors of the dead; my love for you has brought me here."

A reply came: "What is the matter with my only son? My love? What evil has befallen you? Why do you call me from beyond the trembling veil?"

He answered: "A cunning woman has advised me to walk towards darkness and danger to seek my destined beloved bride, the beautiful Menglad."

The mother said: "The longings of the living are endless but if your will is raised, I will call for the wisdom of the witches to make it happen, for you to meet your beloved."

"Sing to me galder-songs that can help me mother. Protect me in my journey into the great darkness and unknown," he pleaded.

"I will sing your triumph galder as Rane sang for Rind. Know this: from the shoulder the arrow flies, be your own judge of manners and be a leader unto yourself.

I sing you a second: if out on the road you shall go without joy, my song will make you upright. Know that the witch's homely enclosure can be found everywhere, even when the ground is barren.

I sing you a third: if the currents are strong within the cascading rivers of conflict, I will reduce their surging waves for you.

I sing you a fourth: when enemies are keen to lead you to the gallows. May their spirit be turned to reconciliation and friendship.

I sing you a fifth: if fetters are to be bound about your arms and legs, let feasting and fellowship unlock your shackles.

I sing you a sixth: may the proud bow of your ship carry you over the high and curved waves of the whale-road.

I sing you a seventh: may your body be kept safe from the sharp frosts and the arrows of hail on the high mountain passes.

I sing you an eighth: a dead Christian woman may not do away with you on the twilight paths.

I sing you a ninth: if you need to boast with your weapons. I sing for common sense and that the feelings of the good heart may be the first and last to strike.

Never go where danger is palpable. When I stood in front of the dark gates, magic songs I carved onto my staff. Carry with you these rune-songs, let them dwell in your chest, happiness and fullness in life you will have, if you remember them."

She then gave him five gifts: a spell for his horse to never tire over land and water; A tablecloth on which food will appear if hunger strikes; a golden drinking-horn which can never empty; a sword named Aldering, hardened in dragon's blood; and a ship that can ride over crested waves and will never sink before enemy ships.

Through many lands he travelled, many kingdoms he helped with his sword, he was unbowed before enemy ships and he travelled to the end of the nine-worlds and arrived at the gates of his beloved.

At the gate of Menglad.

Svipdag faced the shining gates. A hooded watchman approached him and said:

"What kind of troll is standing outside the golden gates, wandering around with a flame of love at heart?"

"What are you looking for and what are you snooping for, friendless and defenseless, what do you want to know?"

Svipdag replied:

"What kind of a troll is standing outside his keep and does not welcome a lonely wanderer? Have you lived a life without praise?"

The watchman answered:

"With a tongue like that you will not find greetings here."

Svipdag replied:

"I would like to enter the full bright gates and visit the golden halls."

The watchman said:

"Tell me, to whom were you born?"

Svipdag said:

"My father's name was Varkald and Fjolkald was his father. Now tell me, watchman, I must ask and wish to know, who rules this realm and who has power and property of these great lavish halls?"

The watchman replied:

"Her name is Menglad; she rules here and has all the power and property."

Svipdag asked:

"Tell me, watchman, I must ask and wish to know, what are these gates called?"

The watchman said:

"The gates are called Trymglol, made by the sons of Solblinde and gold is forever bestowed to the one who travels through them."

Svipdag said:

"Tell me, watchman, I must ask and wish to know – what is the name of the high boundary of this realm?"

The watchman said:

"Gastropner is the name of the boundary and it is made from the clay giant's limbs – the boundary will stand high until the giants ride over the rainbow bridge."

Svipdag said:

"Tell me, watchman, I must ask and want to know, what are the names of these hungry hounds that are heard barking beyond the gates?"

The watchman replied:

"One is called Givr and the other Gere, if you want to know."

Svipdag asked:

"Tell me, watchman, I must ask and wish to know, must a man enter only when such beasts are asleep?"

The watchman said:

"Uneven sleep guards their domain; one wolf sleeps at night, the other during the day. They are always watchful.

Svipdag said:

"Tell me, watchman, I must ask and wish to know, is there any food in those high halls for mortals to eat?"

The watchman said:

"If you want to know, the only food you require here is found in the tail-feathers of the wind-hawk."

Svipdag asked:

"Tell me, watchman, I must ask and wish to know, what is the tree called, which spreads its branches over all people and the gods, goddesses and giants?"

The watchman answered:

"It is called Mimameidr, but none knows where the roots go. It grows from somewhere that few can imagine; the tree cannot be struck down by flame or iron."

Svipdag said:

"Tell me, watchman, I must ask and wish to know, what fruit does the high-tree bear as it cannot be felled by flames or iron?"

The watchman said:

"From its acorn leaps a flame to help women who suffer in secret and in childbirth, the flame burns over outwards and reveals what inwardly is hidden, it also burns within men."

Svipdag enquired:

"Tell me, watchman, I must ask and wish to know, who is the cockerel who sits in the high tree, glowing of gold?"

The watchman informed him:

"His name is Wind-hawk. In the wind his feathers glow on the tree's twigs. He bestows angst to Surt Sinmara."

Svipdag said:

"Tell me, watchman, I must ask and wish to know, what weapon can be used to reach the halls of the deepest Hel-hem below?"

The watchman said:

143

"The weapon is named Lävatei. Lopt forged it with runes written on the doors of death. In Lägjarn's casket it lies with Sinmara, but it is enclosed by nine strong locks."

Svipdag said:

"Tell me, watchman, I must ask and wish to know, can a man ever hope to return who tries to win this weapon?"

The watchman said:

"He who turns away greed may take the steel, but only if he brings back the sickle to the shining goddess of gold."

Svipdag said:

"Tell me, watchman, I must ask and wish to know, what treasure makes the great giantess gentle?"

The watchman said:

"The sickle is found within the wind-hawk's feathers. Give it to Sinmara and she will bless a weapon to be born."

Svipdag asked:

"Tell me, watchman, I must ask and wish to know, what is the name of the hall which is closed by magic flames?"

The watchman answered:

"That noble house is called Lyr and long and sharp are the spear-flames."

Svipdag said:

"Tell me, watchman, I must ask and wish to know, who were the gods that made the halls great to behold?"

The watchman said:

"Une and Ire, Bare and Ore, Var and Vegdrasil, Dore and Ure, Delling and Loki; the fear of the folk."

Svipdag said:

"Tell me, watchman, I must ask and wish to know, what is the mountain called, whereupon the bride sits high in her glory?"

The watchman said:

"Lyfjaberg it is called and long shall it be a joy to the sick and the sore. Health shall grow in each woman who climbs it, even though she has lain sick for long."

Svidag questioned:

"Tell me, watchman, I must ask and wish to know, what maidens are they that sit gladly at Menglad's knees?"

The watchman replied:

"One is called Liv, the other Livtrasa, the third known as Tjodvarta, Bjort and Blid, Blid and Frid, Eir and Aurboda."

Svipdag said:

"Tell me, watchman, I must ask and wish to know. Do they bring aid in exchange of offerings or when need is given?"

The watchman said:

"They help the wise to give, if they are offered sacrifices in the place where the high altar stands. They guard us from illness."

Svipdag said:

"Tell me, watchman, I must ask and wish to know, is there a man who can sleep happily in Menglad's arms?"

The watchman said:

"There is no man who can sleep happily in Menglad's arms, except Svipdag alone; the bride on the mountain to him is destined."

Svipdag said:

"Up with the doors! Open the gate! Here you can see Svipdag. Go and ask if Menglad is glad to receive me."

The watchman said:

"Do you hear, Menglad, a man has come here. The dogs greet him, the gates have opened; it seems as if he is Svipdag."

Menglad said:

"On the gallows high, hungry ravens will pluck your eyes if you lie saying that at last the hero has come to my hall. Where have you been? Where did you travel from? What do you call a home? An emblem I must know if I am destined to be your bride."

Svipdag said:

"Svipdag is my name, Solbjart was my father's name; away they drove me on cold roads and high winds. No-one can resist the onslaught of fate, even if happiness does not become our lot."

Menglad said:

"I am happy you have now come; my longing is met. I greet you with a loving kiss! My love and delight. Long have I sat on Lyfjaberg, the healing mountain, waiting for you, day by day – and now I have all that I ever hoped for, for you my love have come to my halls!

Alike we yearn and I longed for you and you for my love have longed: now together we know our lives and when it seems like the end, we shall live together."

YOUR SOUL AS BELOVED

In this world and in the mythic imagination, there is a mystery that pervades all relationships and all actions: romantic love. Romantic love is an arrow with swan feathers that appears from the blue sky and shakes life to its innermost. In Greece, this love-arrow is shot from the bow of Eros and all gods fear it. In the north, it lies within the heartbeat of Freya. The Greek world had many names for many other aspects of love, names such as: Philia (kinship and family) or Ludus (being amongst friends) and Pragma (maturing love) or Agape (unconditional love) and Philautia (self-love).

Many religious traditions speak of transforming the power of Eros into the direction of other aspects of love as mentioned above – not an easy proposition when the love that is mostly highlighted in our society is the one that includes a sexual partner and all the foolish and uncontrollable liveliness. This is a primal psychic energy that makes up most of our art and music. This love is not some minor deity; it stands at the very centre of our life-force. Our world is erotic – erotic in every blade of grass and behind every motion. To deny this love is to deny nature herself.

The arrows of Eros can hurt: families can be displaced, communities torn apart and entire kingdoms reduced to ashes. Helen's face launched a thousand ships to the city of Troy. The irresistible force of romantic love is a dangerous energy for the structures of society and a life in bloom and has always been concealed and locked up within cultural taboos. We do not "rise" into this kind of love when we are shot by Eros, or see a glimpse of Freya's magical hair; we "fall" into love when struck – treacherous waters are stirred and the plot always thickens – a journey has begun.

When Orpheus falls in love, he takes the first steps towards the trembling veil between this world and another; first in elation and then in anguish. His journey stands in the opposite direction to Icarus; his is a downward journey, the serpent journey. Svipdag is harnessed to his horse to look for his beloved away from home towards the otherworld and the world of the dead. The curious troll moves through dark space for hundreds of years with a magic sickle reaching for the Moon.

Many stories and myths bestow love and a full redemption, it crowns the created cosmos. Orpheus, through his music and his endeavours, raises love above the cold hand of death as he joins Eurydice in the immortal lands. This love, when felt deeply enough, can lead us to the blessed isles, but only if we are prepared to go through the tortuous paths that love leads us down, to ride to the very gates or to take the journey to the Moon and back. We are asked to hold our precious love as the wolves howl and close in on us.

Orpheus offers his music to the dawn, a libation of beauty to the creation around him.

Alchemy suggests dawn to be a moment that is split between heaven and earth, and in that split – consciousness is born. The dawning of the day becomes the birth of consciousness as well as the triumph of light over dark. This myth is retold by the Sun every 24 hours as it reveals the landscape and paints it with its divine light.

In music we often hear the original unity of creation and Orpheus seeks that which stands behind his music; he wants to see the one that drives him to create his melodies. The etymology of the word music comes from the word mousikē (art) of the Muses, from mousa meaning "muse". In ancient Greece, artists would call and invoke their "muse" before any performance. Orpheus wanders through the wilds of Greece to seek his muse, to seek the one who is the foundation of his art. He happens to come across the river nymphs; the word nymph in Greek also means "bride". Upon seeing Eurydice, his fate is sealed and his heart receives a sovereign queen, which is reciprocal in Eurydice as she receives him as her king (anima and animus joined).

The inner sovereignty of love can be terrifying if it is not met with reciprocal terms. How many of us have not laid awake possessed with the idea of loving someone who has no interest in loving us back? Many have to endure this cruelty of Eros' arrows. Eros aimed right for both of them, and what follows is the elation that love brings: a joy which shakes the silken tapestries of the gods themselves. As a blossoming cherry tree, their joy is short-lived when the terrible separation strikes: the fangs in the grass bite into Eurydice's heel, and all the joy and elation that was with Orpheus is now transformed into an ocean of smouldering ash. He has to enter the labyrinth, the serpent path, to reclaim his life and love. Just as the curios troll takes the flight to the moon-mountains.

Notice in the Orpheus myth how we are introduced to the image of the serpent in the beginning of the story. When this transformation strikes, we have to journey down to find our soul again. The idea of losing the memory of Eurydice strikes fear into Orpheus. In the Poetic Edda Odin says:

> *"Hugin and Munin fly over the whole Earth every morning. I fear that Hugin (thought) will never return, but for Munin (memory) I fear more"*
>
> (Trans. Andreas Kornevall).

When we stand in front of the gates, guardians appear – they are all that hold us back: Grief, Anxiety, Disease, Old Age, Fear, Hunger, Death, Agony, and Sleep. Are they also our protectors, those that keep us in life's realm?

Our psychology has not changed since this story has been told. We wield nuclear weapons with the same mindset that wielded our bronze swords back then – we have not evolved psychologically; the stories, therefore, told in the Bronze Age or Viking Age, have the same psychological truth and insight that concerns us today – their imagery speaks directly to our present time. This soul journey to find love was as relevant then as it is today. The knowledge that this psychological journey exists cannot be learnt academically, this path insists on the subjective experience, the initiation.

Once in the underworld, Orpheus goes through the orchard of rotting fruit, revealing the nature of death and decay, which is followed by nearly drowning in the overwhelming depths of the waters: the rivers of tears that spring from each eye in the world, and the rivers of blood from all battles and conflict. The third brother in the waters of life bends his head when arriving at the bridge arching over the river and there receives hard-earned gifts from the dwarf.

In northern myth, the deep loss of a loved one, the tears, are usually seen as a transformation from grief into something precious. They celebrate the depth of soul that was reached through the loving relationship when it was alive. When Freya weeps, her tears touch water and they turn into amber and when they touch the earth they are transformed into gold, giving us an image of permanent value in an otherwise transient world that is losing its sense of fidelity.

Orpheus is given a chance to bring his beloved back on one condition: he must not turn back as they walk through the Valley of Death, or else the concession they are being offered will count for nothing. But his doom lingers and he fails. He turns before the Sun shines upon his brow. Eurydice is swept back into the tenebrous caves and he loses her for the second time. He is now "twice bereaved" – a fate which leaves him as a nightingale singing through his sorrow across the river. Upon walking out of Hades, he is a changed man who can now see all the sufferings of the word. With his broken heartbeat, he makes even more miraculous music; this is the pinnacle of the teachings of this wisdom: he does not fall into despair, but returns to the world of the living and crafts beauty from his sorrow. This is true magic, taking difficult emotions and transforming them into beauty. As the curios troll is blinded by the light, he still stands firm and protects his sunbeam from the hungry wolves.

Orpheus makes such beauty that women from all the corners of the world feel as if the music is for them alone, for each of their own hearts, they are unable to share their love for Orpheus and their love for him turns irrepressible: they must have him. How many people that we put up on the great stages of the world suffer a similar fate? Here love becomes an obsession, which results in his death, and now not even his music can save him; his fate is sealed. He joins the drifting ghosts of the dead.

Persephone, whom Homer describes as "... the formidable, venerable majestic princess of the underworld ..." is the personification of green shoots rising from the ashes, that which opens the wells of fertility and all that which carries sheer potentiality. In the spring season, she is a custodian for that which is regenerative and restorative. Only memories can recall the self, and with Orpheus and Eurydice, their memories have ceased and are receding into the underworld where time has lost its purpose. From the Well of Memory, they are enabled to see again, we do not know from Ovid's "Metamorphoses" whether this is Persephone who has felt pity to intervene, but their souls flow with life-giving waters and open into the undying lands. They are reunited by their love and in their existential victory over forgetfulness and death. This is the authentic seeing. The collection of memories into the well that feeds life – the Tree of Life.

Romantic love is a fierce arrow and if we are to follow our hearts, the stories show us that the journey is a descent of difficulties, passing through many emotional zones, but in the end it's a journey that leads to our own soul – our beloved.

CHAPTER 8

Mysteries of the Northern Sky – Remembering

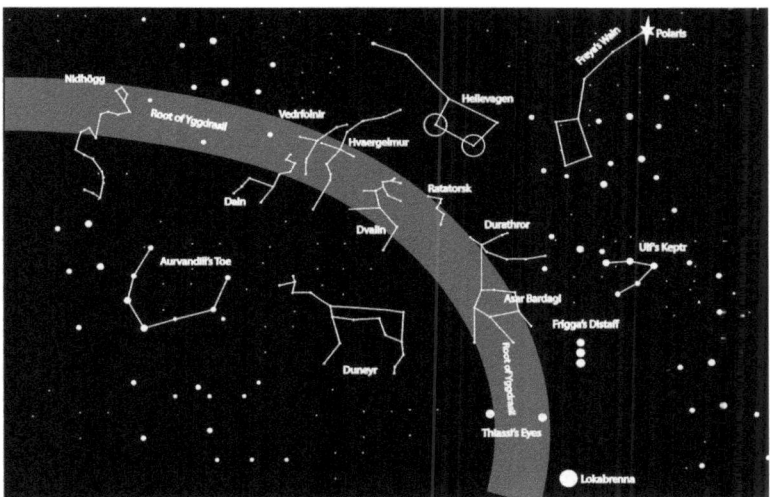

NORTHERN STAR CONSTELLATIONS

"Why did not someone teach me the constellations and make me a home in the starry heavens, which are always overhead and which I don't half know to this day?"

Thomas Carlyle's Lament

There is a deep vacancy in our starry-imaginations and in the northern history of celestial interpretation. Much of what we know of the northern constellations is based on guesswork, pieced together in source material or rebuilt through personal gnosis. But this makes the work fulfilling; we are turning over old tombs, entering the unknown and imagining how our ancestors interpreted the great sparkling earth roof at night.

I would encourage you to imagine and develop these further.

1. Thiassi's Eyes

The two Gemini stars, Castor and Pollux, resemble two eyes as they have a similar brightness in the skies. You can see them very clearly in the month of January. Thiassi was a giant related to winter and to the Apples of Immortality. The trickster Loki was once forced by Thiassi to trick Idunn (the goddess who carries the basket of apples) out of Asgard. In the form of an eagle, Thiassi snatched Idunn from the wood and took her to his home. Her absence made the gods grow old and grey.

Loki had to journey on a great quest to bring the apples back, his disguise as a hawk led him to the chamber where Idunn was kept prisoner and through his spell-craft he turned her into a walnut and brought her back to Asgard. Thiassi, finding out he has been outwitted by Loki, takes an eagle shape and chases Loki in the skies – the chase from where all storm winds are born. Seeing the furious dogfight overhead, the gods make a fire with high leaping flames and as soon Thiassi crosses their ramparts, his feathers catch fire like "dried grass in summer" and the gods kill him in his untimely descent.

In chapter 56 of the Prose Edda book, "Skáldskaparmál", Thiassi's daughter, Skadi, puts on her helmet and carries "all weapons of war" and travels to Asgard for a bloodied revenge. The gods receive her and offer her compensation for the killing that was done. Skadi agrees to the deal with two provisions – first; she can choose a husband amongst the gods, and second; they must make her laugh again. To this the gods agree – however, there is one condition in return: she must choose her husband by looking only at the gods' feet. Skadi agrees to the game and finds two white feet particularly attractive. The owner of the feet turns out to be Njord, the God of the Coastal Waters.

Then Loki ties one end of a cord around the beard of a goat and the other end around his testicles. It all goes wrong for Loki and he starts squealing loudly and suddenly Skadi laughs. Finally, in compensation to Skadi, during the wedding ceremony, Odin takes Thiassi's bright eyes and creates two stars.

2. Duneyr (Drooping-ears)

One of the first deer constellations.

> "Four harts also
> The highest shoots,
> They gnaw from beneath:
> Dáin and Dvalin,
> Duneyr and Dýrathrór"
>
> Poetic Edda.

3. Durathror (Sluggish Beast)

The stars are from the Greek/Roman Perseus constellation as its head and antlers and the Auriga constellation is the body.

4. Dvalin (Sleeper)

Another deer constellation. Consists of some of the same stars as Cepheus.

5. Dain

Dáinn, deer constellation.

Dain, Dvalin, Duneyr and Durathror. Dain and Dvalin are described in the Eddas, "… as if they are living in a mist." Note their position on the roots of Yggdrasil.

More lost stag constellations?

Two animals stand on the roof of Valhalla (the abode of the gods): the goat Heidrun and the deer Eiktyrner, and they feed from the branches and they give back gifts to the Tree. The goat offers mead and the deer pours water from its antlers into the roots. They are both said to live in balance with the Tree. Some more investigation is needed for this for later publication.

6. Ratatosk (Gnaw-tooth)

The squirrel constellation. Consists of the main stars in Cassiopeia.

Prose Edda: The squirrel called Ratatosk runs up and down the ash. He tells slanderous gossip, provoking the eagle and Nidhogg.

7. Hvaergelmur

The eagle constellation is similar to Cygnus the Swan.

> *He is called Hræsvelg,*
> *who sits at heaven's end,*
> *a giant, in the shape of an eagle;*
> *from his wings*
> *They say the wind comes over all people.*
>
> "Vafþrúðnismál" – trans. J. Lindow (2002, 37).

8. *Vedrfolnir (Wind-parched)*

Constellation for the hawk upon the eagle's head.

Edda: There is much to be told. An eagle sits at the top of the ash, and it has knowledge of many things. Between its eyes sits the hawk called Vedrfolnir.

9. *Hellewagen*

> *"We know that in the very earliest ages the seven stars forming the Bear in the northern sky were thought of as a four-wheeled wagon, its pole being formed by the three stars that hang downwards."*
>
> Grimm (2004: 151).

Hellewagen – constellation of the wagon of the dead, that travels upon the Milky Way down to the underworld.

These words were carved on the statue of Thor at Uppsala:

> *The God Thor was the highest of them,*
> *He sat naked as a child,*
> *Seven stars in his hand and Charles's Wain.*

In some part of northern Europe, this was also known as "Óðinsvagn" (Odin's wagon), a kenning to support this is "Valdrvagnbrautar" (ruler of the wagon road) proposing the "wagon road" as was the heavens, the Allfather – the ruler of the heavens.

The Dutch used Woonswaghen or Woenswaghen, the seven stars of Wotan's Wagon, another clear indicator as Ursa Major has seven stars.

10. Nidhogg (Poison-biter)

Constellation of a serpent at the foot of Yggdrasill's root.

> *Yggdrasil's ash*
> *hardship suffers*
> *greater than men know of;*
> *a hart bites it above,*
> *and in its side it rots,*
> *Nidhögg tears it.*
>
> Grímnismál (35).

11. The Roots of Yggdrasil

The white chalk that glimmers and stands above heaven and *"no-one knows where the roots run to."*

Odin, Poetic Edda.

12. Aurvandill's Toe

Snorri Sturluson records in the Skáldskaparmál:

> *"Thórr went home to Thrúdvangar, and the whetstone remained sticking in his head. Then came the wise woman who was called Gróa, wife of Aurvandill the Valiant: she sang her spells over Thórr until the stone was loosened. But when Thórr knew that, and thought that there was hope that the whetstone might be removed, he desired to reward Gróa for her leech-craft and make her glad, and told her these things: that he had waded from the north over the River Élivága (icy stream) and had borne Aurvandill in a basket on his back from the north out of Jôtunheim. And he added for a token, that one of Aurvandill's toes had stuck out of the basket, and became frozen; wherefore Thórr broke it off and cast it up into the heavens, and made thereof the star called Aurvandill's Toe.*

Thórr said that it would not be long ere Aurvandill came home: but Gróa was so rejoiced that she forgot her incantations, and the whetstone was not loosened, and stands yet in Thórr's head. Therefore, it is forbidden to cast a whetstone across the floor, for then the whetstone is stirred in Thórr's head."

This constellation is the same as the Corona Borealis, which is also the indicator of spring as it is seen during spring and summer in the Northern Hemisphere, and it also looks like a toe.

13. *Frigga's Distaff*

Friggerock (Frigg's Distaff) – the stars that make up the belt of Orion. As it has a vertical orientation, it can be seen as a spindle. In Sweden, it is called Friggerock. The constellation is now called Mariärock or, in Danish, Marirock (Magnusen, gloss. 361, 376), "the Christians having passed the same old idea on to Mary, the heavenly mother" (Grimm, 2004: 270). The whole constellation could be a representation of the goddess herself.

14. *Ulf's Keptr*

The giant wolf, Fenrir, together with Hel and the World Serpent, is a child of Loki and the Giantess Angrboda. Known as Ulf's Keptr (the Mouth of the Wolf) – the wolf guards the gates of the underworld, and the stars form a V shape, like the jaws of the wolf.

15. *Asar Bardagi*

This is actually the constellations on the body of Durathror, named as the battlefield of the gods, with the wolf stalking nearby.

16. *Freya's High Seat*

The Ursa Minor. The constellation of Freya's High Seat, where she sits and the polar star adorns her throne.

17. *Lokabrenna*

The brightest star: Sirius. This star was known as the Torch of Loki. When it twinkles, it can be said that Loki is active in the world – a time of the trickster.

HIDDEN RUNE KNOWLEDGE OF THE STARS

Professor Sigurd Agrell dedicated most of his life to trying to uncover the magical and non-linguistic significance of the runes to regain some of the knowledge that we had lost. His analysis of the runes offers many layers of meaning.

What he set out to study first was the sequential listing of the rune alphabet itself; this is the basic A to Z, and to find out how the runic letters were organized. The rune-row and sequence can only be found in three places: the Kylver Stone, the Vadstena Bracteate and the Grumpan Bracteate. When we approach these talismans and carvings, something unexpected happens and here lies the first part of Professor Agrell's uncovering: when you look closely at the Kylver Stone rune-row, the runes have a different sequence of letters than the other amulets. For example, on the Kylver Stone the rune ODAL is the last rune and on the Vadstena and Grumpan Bracteates the rune DAGAZ is the last – both runes have shifted positions. Comparatively, it would be as if suddenly the Y was listed after Z in our own alphabet. Today, scholars regard the bracteates as a more reliable source as they were "stamped" into the amulets and worn by people, whereas the Kylver Stone was carved by hand by one individual and it looks as if it was done in haste, but we cannot be sure of this discrepancy.

Ancient Gods

The bracteates were imitations of the Emperor coins of late antiquity. To illustrate this further, on the Vadstena Bracteate you find the head of a horned bull and, behind it, the head of man – in late antiquity this was the symbol of the God Meithra next to a sacrificial bull. The God Meithra was affiliated with Roman soldiers and called the "unconquerable god" – his bracteate would have been worn by soldiers for protection when they went into battle and these bracteates were worn late into the Christian era. Many German soldiers served in the Roman armies and the Emperor Commodus himself was an initiate of the Meithras religion which increased in numbers amongst officials and soldiers. The northern bracteate's relationship to the late antiquity coin is clear to understand simply by the naked eye: they are identical in design.

On the Vadstena Bracteate, apart from the rune-row script which reveals the row of letters, there is also an incantation stamped on it which spells out: "tuwatuwa". Now, Prof. Agrell started to examine if he could find a cypher and discover some underlying magical formula within this incantation. He proceeded to give each rune a number according to its position in the FUTHARK rune row. To reiterate, the FUTHARK rune row is the A to Z of the rune alphabet. In his method, the rune F would represent the number 1, just like A would represent 1 in our alphabet; the rune Uruz would represent 2; rune Thurs would be 3 and so on, up to the last rune, Dagaz for 24.

When he calculated and multiplied all the runes in tuwatuwa, he found them to be: 17+2+8+4+17+2+8+4=62. A disappointing number as it was not affiliated to any magical number symbolism or pattern that he could understand.

However, Prof. Agrell was aware that most of the magical formulas were hidden from the uninitiated, something that is practiced in all occult circles worthy of the name, so why would it be different with the runes? In paradox, due to the failure in seeing a clear magical pattern from the incantation, he started to believe that the Futhark rune row must be a cipher to confuse and hide the inner meaning of the tuwatuwa incantation.

After much researching and mixing the rune-rows around for a long period of time without result, he finally ended up removing the first rune Fehu and put it in the very last position; which revealed a new rune-row, now named the Uthark, with Uruz taking the first place. He used the same concept that we see on a deck of playing cards (which also has divinatory roots). For those who play card games, you may have noticed that when the ace card is in the pack it is the lowest number and counted as number one, but as soon as any game is played, the ace suddenly transforms and becomes the highest scoring card. In a similar way, he took the incantation of tuwatuwa and calculated it again using the Uthark rune-row, and it revealed: $16+1+7+3+16+1+7+3=54$.

In ancient numerology and according to Prof. Agrell, this reveals the number for the God Meithra.

Significant Numbers

The number also points to Abraxas, according to his research, as his name symbolized the sphere of the amulet. Suddenly his discovery, although esoteric, opened many doors towards new associations and symbolic meanings – too many to spell out here, but I will bring to attention some revealing examples:

Firstly, anyone speaking Scandinavian languages will know that the word "Ur" means beginning, Ur-tid (the beginning of time)

Ur-folket (the first peoples) – a properly fitting attribute to the "first" rune now Ur-uz. Also, in German it is Ur-knall (big bang) or Urzeit (the primeval time). In the Semitic old alphabets, they begin by the letter Aleph, which was called ox, or cattle – the etymology of this word comes from the Greek alphabet's first letter "A" – called alpha. Thurs, rune number two, has the meaning of "troll, thurs" – the number 2 has been regarded as the demonic number: diabolo, duality, conflict. The rune Ansuz has now the value 3, which he called to represent the trinity of the three gods: Odin, Vile and Ve.

Moreover, the one association that is noteworthy in particular is the famous rune sequence I mentioned earlier: ALU – the symbols represent the runes Ansuz, Laguz and Uruz, and when you associate ALU with its new "Uthark" numbers, you disclose: (Ansuz for 3, Lagu for 20, and Ur for 1) 3+20+1=24: the total number of runes for the whole rune-row, making the three runes potent magically and desirable in rune carvings.

Again and again, we meet this combination to get to the number 24 in magical carvings. For example, in the Lindholm Amulet we get other runes underlying with the number 24, such as 8 Ansuz runes 3x8=24, or 3 Tiwaz runes 16x3=48 which is 2x24. The numerical value of all the runes cut into the entire amulet is 216 – this includes the number 24 nine times; what's more, the number of runes on the amulet is 24.

In my own research, I stumbled upon how the number 216 was used in Darren Aronofsky's film Pi, the main character found a hidden code in the Universe which was a 216 digit number. But aside from a fictional film, the concept of a 216-letter name of God is revealed from existent Jewish belief. The 216-letter name of God – the Shem HaMephorash – is extracted from three verses (19, 20 & 21) in Exodus: each verse being 72 letters long

(72x3=216). Another interesting point which should not go without mentioning is that when you multiply 6x6x6, you arrive at a total of 216.

The Raido rune now becomes number four: Raido has an etymological meaning of carriage/chariot and here we get a striking conformity with the Meithras symbol of the four-horse carriage, whose holy number is four. Thor was also called the "Chariot God" in Norse mythology. Devotees in his sanctuary in Trondheim always offered him "four" pieces of bread. He was also the protector of the "four" directions.

The whole Uthark rune-row now has new associations and each one of them Prof. Agrell highlights through his work and study.

The craftsmanship and skill of those who made these amulets would have been highly developed in the magic of number symbology. Prof. Agrell in his studies also practiced "gematria" which is the Kabbalistic method of interpreting scriptures by computing the numerical value of ancient words and names, similar to what I referred to earlier. One evening he conducted an experiment with the numerological and magical tools he had at his disposal of the famous number 666.

He summarized the numerology of the names of the Roman Emperors (through their original names in scripture): Nero, Galba, Otho, Vitellius, Vespasianus, Titus and Domitianus and the summary number of their original names, using this ancient method of numerology, he claimed was 616. He argued through his findings that 616 was an alternative number and as recent as 2005, long after his passing, a fragment of Papyrus 115 was revealed, containing the earliest known version of that part of the Book of Revelation and where it was discussing the "Number of the Beast" – it disclosed the number 616 as the original number.

What Professor Agrell shows us is that when manipulating symbols such as the runes and their underlying meaning we are thrown into many associative possibilities. In history, we have been driven to the use of symbols to explain a chthonic reality, a reality revealed by the symbol. In the case of modern science, we use numbers to quantify and prove a thesis, numbers make it credible – numbers exist as powerful symbols to point to a reality. When the ancient magicians conducted their spells, they added the numbers behind the sign and gave it a symbolic wholeness and meaning.

But as it is with much material relating to magical writings and practices, it is impossible to have a clear overview of all this, it stays occult (hidden) after all and that is where it will always remain. However, the fragments we are left with point to a large piece of our ancient history – a history that is fascinating to explore and I am sure many new findings will take place in the future.

Comparative Studies

What happens when we do a comparative study of these multiples as seen in the Uthark rune-row?

To recap: we have 24, 54, 72, 108, 216, 360 and 432.

What we find is a root from the old mystery schools. Many of these numbers have added zeros attached to them, behold the following elegance:

In Norse myth, during what is called the "the Age of the Wolf," 800 warriors will pass through 540 doors: 800x540=32,000.

Number 432 (2x216) is also known in the Hindu idea of cycles of time:

Kali Yuga is said to last for 432,000 years.

10,800 bricks in the Indian Fire Altar.

10,8000 stanzas in the Rigveda, the most ancient of the Vedic Sanskrit texts.

Kabbalah: 72 Angels.

Rosicrucians speak of cycles of 108 years.

Chines Triads – an initiate pays 360 coins for making clothes, 108 for the purse, 72 for instruction.

The ten Christian patriarchs ruled between the rise of the city of Kish and the Great Flood, a period of 432,000 years.

Ancient Chinese volumes written down in a great text: 4,320 volumes.

Mythical Kings of Babylon ruled for 432,000 years.

In Sumer, the time between creation and great catastrophe was 2,160,000 years.

Mayans in Mesoamerica, their long count calendar had times such as the 1 katun=7,200 days; 1 Tun=360 days; 2 Tuns=720 days; 5 Baktuns=720,000 days; 5 Katuns=36,000 days; 6 Katuns =43,200 days; 6 Tuns=2160 days; 15 Katuns=2,160,000 days.

The Rigveda – there are 10,800 stanzas in the Rigveda, the most ancient of the Vedic texts. Each stanza is made of 40 syllables with the result that the entire composition contains 432,000 syllables – no more or less.

What is the origin of these symbolic numbers that appear in the runes and in myths around the world?

It has been observed that certain ancient myths, sacred texts and ancient buildings have "stored" within them common and repeating numerical values and dimensions which relate to an astronomical phenomena.

This knowledge appears to be based on the observation of the precession of the equinoxes.

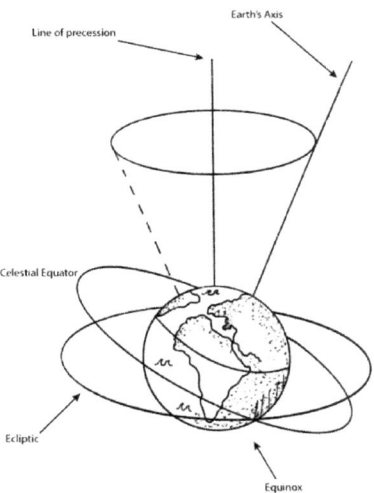

How does it work?

The precession of the equinoxes refers to an observable phenomena of the rotation of the heavens and the cycle that spans a period of (approximately) 25,920 years, over which time the constellations appear to slowly rotate around the Earth, taking turns at rising behind the rising Sun on the vernal equinox.

What are the numbers relating to the processions?

The precession of the equinoxes: 25,920 years = (360° rotation)

If the sky is divided into twelve constellations: 25,920/12=2,160 (note: 6x10x6=360, and 360x6=2,160).

A new sign appears on the horizon every 2,160 years (30°) (note: 2x2,160 or 12 x360=4,320 years).

Therefore, to move 1° on the horizon = 72 years (approximately).

Here we have them:

12, 24, 54, 72, 108, 216 and 432.

Highly significant is of course 216, as it takes 2,160 years to move from one zodiac to the next.

Constellations:

Leo (Lion)	**10,800–8,640 BC**
Cancer (Crab)	**8,640–6,480 BC**
Gemini (Twins)	**6,480–4,320 BC**
Taurus (Bull)	**4,320–2,160 BC**
Aries (Ram)	**2,160 BC–0**
Pisces (Fish)	**0–2,160 AD**
Aquarius (Water Jug)	**2,160–4,320 AD**

I am not sure this was something Prof. Agrell was aware of when he started to uncover the Uthark rune row – he never mentioned it in his texts or sources, which makes the link outside of the statistical spheres and purely magical.

From these numbers we can draw this conclusion in confidence: knowing about the precession of the equinoxes reveals that the ancients understood our star-lit cosmos far more than we give them credit for, and the runes still carry this ancient knowledge within them, but only when the Uthark rune-row is revealed – make a note that none of these numbers would be made visible when we use the Futhark rune row.

CHAPTER 9

Hel'sRoad–MythCycle[*]

THE THIRD MYTH CYCLE – THE ROAD TO HEL

Balder was born from Odin and Frigg The God of Poetry and the Goddess of the Waters. He was the most loved of all the gods as his cheerful nature was believed to stop even Ragnarok itself –

[*] From a traditional remembrance rune stone in Sweden, called the U460 stone.

the end of the world. Wherever he went, the grief of the gods would come to rest and his words would give comfort.

This was a golden time for the gods and the nine worlds were in peace and contentment.
This was not to last as Balder, in the middle of the night, would begin to have dreams of a grey world. A world filled with tragedy and dying, where compassion was replaced by anger.

He woke from his sleep.

These dreams tormented him for many moons. The gods and goddesses were worried and decided to hold a parliament to discuss this bad omen that had risen in the mind of Balder, and to find out how this night-wraith could have entered the world of the gods. They gathered on the great flowering plains of Hela. There the mighty discussed the dreams and tried to see into the threads of fate and the runes for why Balder received such troubling dreams.

Frigg decided to go and wander the nine worlds and make all the minerals, plants, trees, seas and fires pledge to spare Balder, to never hurt or cause harm to him, and all living things agreed. This powerful magic from Frigg was entertaining to the gods and they would throw a stone and observe how it would land before it hit him. They tried with spears and arrows, which would swerve or stop whenever they came near him – Balder was always left unharmed.

However, runes of sorrow had been weaved into the cloth of fate that Odin alone could see and he wanted some answers – the one-eyed god saddled his horse.

Over the nine worlds he crossed on this eight-legged steed, Sleipner, and his path was headed downwards to the misty land of Hel, the land of the dead. When he finally arrived by the gates, he met the Hel-hound, guardian of the dreaded abyss, whose chest was covered in the blood of the dying. He barked at Odin, the Valfather, who continued and passed him, the hooves of his horse resounded as he galloped into the high road of Hel. Then he rode up to the eastern gate where he knew of a grave mound. When he arrived, he took to his staff and hit the ground calling down into the grave whilst he started to sing old spell-songs, songs to stir the grave of a dead witch; the Volva. His incantations forced the spirit to rise from her sleep. Then she spoke: "Long I have been under the stones and grass, who is this stranger calling at my door, forcing me to wake from the long sleep of the dark?"

Odin replied: "I am only that of a simple wanderer who needs tidings from Hel. Please hear my question, for whom have you prepared the banquet of food and adorned the benches and crowned with gold?"

The witch replied: "The mead and food is brewed and cooked for Balder. But I have no wish to rise into this living world, I wish to be undisturbed and return to my silence."

Odin replied and lifted his staff: "Do not be silent, tell me this, how will Balder meet his end in the world of the gods?"

The witch replied: "That which is blind will strike Balder."

Odin said: "Who will avenge his death and bring justice?"

The witch replied: "Rind will give life to Vali in the halls of the west, where Sol sets, the son of Odin will fight when born, he will bring to the pyre the enemy, now let me rest under the stones."

Odin replied: "Do not rest yet, let me ask you one more question, who are the girls that will weep for love and who will throw their flower garlands up to the sky?"

The witch replied: "You are no simple wanderer; you are Odin, the one who receives sacrifices!"
Odin replied, "You are not the witch, nor a wise woman, you are the Mother of Death and Greed!

She spat and yelled, "Ride home Odin, you have won great renown in the world, but time moves towards Hel and you will also return here in the half-light when the fetters of the world are broken asunder when the time of Ragnarok comes."

During the time when Odin was in misty Hel looking for answers, Loki was seized by a jealous fever. He hated the light of Balder as it shone and how the gods adored him.

He concocted an insidious plan.

He changed his shape to an old woman and walked towards the watery temples of Frigg. There Frigg, unaware, greeted the old woman amongst her vitreous lakes and shimmering dew ponds. Under her arched temple, the old woman spoke: "Dear Frigg, have you witnessed how they are all playing this game of attacking poor Balder and each time he is unharmed?"

Frigg responded: "No sword, spear or axe may hurt him; all have taken oaths to me to leave him free from harm." The old woman asked, "Is there really nothing at all that can hurt Balder, as it worries me so to see it?"

There is a plant that grows from the eastern slopes of Valhalla, it is named mistletoe and it was spared as it was too young, feeble and tender to make the pledge."

The old woman turned away and left Frigg's water-temple.

Loki went out into the forest and to the hills west of Valhalla and there gathered the mistletoe plant and with his jealous fingers started to craft a sharp arrow from its stalk, devious and cunning runes were carved into the stalk of the mistletoe.

He waited for the time to be right, for the game to be played again and when the gods gathered during a festive day, he brought his bow and arrow along with him. There one of the Gods launched a spear towards Balder and everyone laughed at how it flew crooked to avoid him; more arrows were fired, Balder didn't mind at all, it was only light-hearted fun – he was allowing their joy to be unhindered.

There up on the grass sat Balder's brother, Hodr, who was blind. Loki went up to him and whispered, "You must feel rather sad not being able to join in the cheerfulness and not be given the opportunity to show Balder the honour of demonstrating his protective power."

The blind god agreed, but shrugged his shoulders and said: "Ah well, I do not see and I am also without a weapon."

"Here," said Loki, "stand up and I will guide you. I will stretch this great bow for you and point this arrow. Hod held the bow and Loki helped him steady himself and he carefully placed the arrow above his hand where he could take aim, then he hunkered down and looked along the straight shaft which pointed right to the chest of beautiful Balder. "Release!" Loki shouted.

The black stick flew in the air and it pierced Balder straight through his heart and he fell down lifeless, killed instantly.

When the gods saw what had happened they tried to speak, or yell, but only their crying could be heard as they bowed their heads. Frigg wept in her temple. Balder had been killed and strewn around him were weapons, swords, spears and axes.

At Balder's funeral the whole mosaic of creation arrived – trolls stood next to elves, giants, tomtar, land-wights, wardens and humans. Frigga was escorted by Odin, then all the valkyries followed behind, two ravens flew high in the skies above. The great Love God Frey arrived drawn on a chariot by the golden boar Gullinbursti, Heimball rode on his mighty steed Gulltop and Freya wore her great tiara and necklace and was pulled by her great cats. All approached and gave their offerings to Balder's ship Hringhorni, where his body was laid. It was a gathering the nine worlds had only seen at the ritual of reconciliations between the Aesir and Vanir. Odin offered his ring, Draupnir, to the ship that contained all the world's wealth and whispered a secret into Balder's ear.

There was also Balder's wife, Nanna – her heart had broken of sorrow and she was laid next to Balder to burn with him in the roaring fire.

The size of his ship was the largest ever built and gifts, torques, shields, spears and jewels filled the ship up to the brim; it was too heavy to push out to sea.

The cries and the laments rose in the air, a wild litany of words and songs, women's tresses were cut, tears flowed towards the ship.

Odin called on his berserkers to step forward to push the ship out from the banks, but to no avail – it was anchored from its sheer weight of gifts on the beach.

Then a giantess stepped forward, named Hyrrokkin, she had arrived to grieve with the gods, riding on a wolf with reins made of serpents. She went to the prow and with one hand pushed the ship, all the lands trembled as the ship left its banks and floated out to the sea. Thor blessed the ship with his hammer and during this blessing a dwarf called Litr ran by his feet and Thor kicked him into the keen flames of the ship.

There all the worlds were present, watching the largest of all funeral fires float to the sea, a bright flickering candle of the world under the sweep of sky, the flame faded as the ship was blown out towards the western horizon. All were distraught and chanting for Balder. They sang of his fairness and graciousness. The air itself sang a lament and black clouds seethed with lightning.

Frigg was unable to be comforted as she sang her grief. She called out to her brave son Hermod to come forward and begged him to take the long road to Hel as a living god, and to bring his brother Balder back from the land of the dead.

Hermod left the world of the gods and for nine nights he rode into dark dales. He reached the River of Gjöll and found the golden tinged Gjöll-bridge that arches over the shadowy water. There stands the maiden Modgudr, who said, "You don't have the colour, nor the heart of a dead man, why are you riding into the Hel-way?"

He said: "I have been selected to find Balder the Beautiful. Have you seen him on this road?"

"Yes," she replied, "he has ridden over the bridge to the other side." Hermod thanked Modgudr and rode on through lands where goblin-shrieks and wolf-howls carried on the wind and mountain ranges were draped in threatening fog. Whirls of ghosts revealed themselves as he came closer to the large gate of the Hel. There he drove his steed forward, the sound of the hooves echoed and his spurs kicked to encourage a leap of faith over the gates and into the underworld. His horse took charge and passed it by a whisker.

Hermod entered large strange halls filled with moonlight, he dismounted from his horse and there met his beloved brother, Balder, sitting on a high seat.

Hermod was invited as an honoured guest for the night.

The next morning he begged Hel, the Goddess of the Dead, if he could bring Balder back to the living. Hel answered, "It would be impossible, but say to the gods above: if all the living things who have learnt not to harm Balder can begin to grieve for him and their tears touch the soil or water, then his light can return – but he must remain here if anyone's eye is dry."

Hermod rose and rode back to Valhalla and told the gods what Hel had instructed.

The gods sent tidings to all the four different quarters and all the plants, trees, metals, minerals and elves, trolls and humans heard the call and their holy water fell from the ground, all could weep for Balder.

One messenger came upon an old woman, just the same one that had visited Frigg's temple, observing him.

He called to her: "Who are you?"

"I am Thökk," she said.

"I have a message from the gods: they want you to grieve for Balder, in order for him to return to the worlds above."

She answered: "I will weep, yes, I will weep. But the tears will be dry; none will fall on the land nor water. If he is living or dead, I don't care. Let Hel hold on to what she has in her halls!"
The messenger left.

The old woman shapeshifted her form and there he stood: Loki, thinking about his crimes, but feeling no remorse.

From then on Loki was in exile from Asgard.

GRIEF – GODDESS OF WATER

This central Norse myth concerns Loki, a trickster god, using an arrow to kill the light, personified in the form of the "beautiful god" Balder, the son of Odin and Frigga. The arrow pierces Balder's heart, he dies and the light slowly fades into the underworld. Such is the grief of the gods that Frigga goes against the laws of the ordered cosmos and sends Hermode, whose name translates as the "courage of thousands," to ride down to the underworld to bargain with Hel, the Goddess of Death, and bring the light back into the world of gods and men.

Hel responds to Hermode's request with a proposed deal: "If everything in the world will grieve for Balder, then I will send him back. But everything must weep: the stones, the rivers, the sky, the trees, animals, men, gods – everything!"

Hermode returns and Frigga hears Hel's instruction. She speaks to all of creation and every stone and sea, all start to grieve for Balder. A depth of love in creation is revealed: a love and compassion that encompasses more than the world of gods and humans, but which includes all the beings in the world – animate and inanimate. But one giantess refuses to cry: "My eyes will be dry for Balder," she says. As long as this giantess refuses to share her tears; nothing can be done to bring Balder back. His light remains imprisoned in the underworld. The name of this giantess is Thokk. Scholar Maria Kvilhaug translates this name as "ungratefulness, unthankfulness."

To have dry eyes for Balder is to deny the world our love and our praise. Today, to have dry eyes in the face of the sixth mass extinction is to refuse Hel's bargain – if we cannot grieve for the loss of the wild places, then were they ever loved?

All of life – mountains, rivers, forests – has a longing for the light to return and it is weeping for its absence.

Entire economies and lifestyles have been created which seem designed to deny this grieving. There are many ways to deny the richness of the living Earth and to look away from its degradation. Ungratefulness has kept the light chained below. We are playing as Loki, tricking ourselves and so denying the world of its rightful light. Under the artificial light of civilization, our shadows have grown deep: the sixth mass extinction, pandemics, climate change and overpopulation.

As the world's rainforests and species diminish like the snows in spring, many are finding themselves in an existential depression. Our emotional response to what is happening with the world and the larger collapse of our climate has not yet begun; the river of tears for Balder is dammed for now. As species are lost after millions of years of evolutionary life, no wreath, no flowers, not even a song has been offered as remembrance. Only science and silence was the response from the world when the Yangtze River dolphin was lost: her obituary was the static sound of radio waves and a tick on an IUCN Red List.

Many phenomenologists, poets and philosophers have claimed that we owe the animals a debt for our ability to read and write, as our skill to read abstract words and figures (as you are doing now) may have evolved from our ability to read the tracks of other creatures moving across the land. If this theory is correct, then there would be no Holy Bible, no Sutra and no Darwin without the bear, the wolf and the deer writing their own poetic tracks across the land for us to read. It can also be theorized that we developed writing by adding their tracks and symbols to our cave walls.

Buried under the soil there are still echoes of our old world; the old stories that connected us to the land are still there. Reclaiming an understanding of the old myths contained in these ancient parchments requires a radical shift of perception. We have been taught to look at myths from a distance. But the Hermode (the courage of thousands) is to be found inside of ourselves, just as is Loki and his self-denial. The myth of Balder asks this question: when were you down there in that underworld carrying a message back from Hel? What have you done with your own grieving? Did you hide it away? Grieving properly can return our humanity back to us and show us where our morality lies, where our inner north star shines. Our grief can reveal to us the value of this precious gift of the spirit in breath and the trees.

The dragon's wisdom roar has been heard across the world since its birth under the feet of the screaming clay-giant. She has been delicately painted on the papyri of Egypt, or carved into the granite rocks of Scandinavia and stroked down with the swirling black ink of Chinese calligraphy.

As a culture, and as individuals, we have become complicit in the death of Balder. Now we must dare to face the underworld, to walk the labyrinth. This is the hard path of transformation: to gain our dragon scales, and, with the offerings and sacrifices that it must entail, to one day find the wisdom for the great Tree to flower.

* * *

Bibliography and Sources

Andrén Anders, et al. Old Norse Religion in Long-Term Perspectives: Origins, Changes, and Interactions: An International Conference in Lund, Sweden, June 3–7, 2004. Nordic Academic Press, 2006.

Ayot, William. Re-Enchanting the Forest: Meaningful Ritual in a Secular World. Sleeping Mountain Press, 2016.

Bates, Brian. The Way of Wyrd: The Book of a Sorcerer's Apprentice. Harper & Row, 1984.

Bauschatz, Paul C. The Well and the Tree: World and Time in Early Germanic Culture. Mass., 1982.

Bly, Robert, et al. The Rag and Bone Shop of the Heart: Poems for Men. HarperCollins, 1993.

Campbell, J. Kudler, D. (2018). Pathways to bliss: Mythology and personal transformation. Yogi Impressions.

Crawford, Jackson. The Poetic Edda. Hackett Publishing Company, Inc, 2015.

Franz, Marie-Luise von. An Introduction to the Interpretation of Fairy Tales. Spring Publications, 1987.

Franz, Marie-Luise von. Problems of the Feminine in Fairytales. Spring Publications, 1972.

Froud, B., Berk, A. (2003). The runes of elfland. Harry N. Abrams.

Hutton, R. (2001). The stations of the sun: A history of the ritual year in Britain. Oxford University Press.

Jung, C.G., Segal, R.A. (1998). Jung on mythology. Princeton University Press.

Karlsson, Thomas. Nightside of the Runes: Uthark, Adulruna, and the Gothic Cabbala. Inner Traditions, 2019.

Kvideland, Reimund, and Henning K. Sehmsdorf. Scandinavian Folk Belief and Legend.

Lindh, C., Höjer Dan, Bauer, J., Moe, L., MasOlle, A., Tenggren, G.A., Norelius, E, Arnold, H. (1997). Bland tomtar och troll: En samling sagor: 1907–1997. Semic AB. Norwegian University Press, 1991.

Kvideland, Reimund. Nordic Folklore: Recent Studies. University Press, 2002.

Kastrup, B. (2016). More than allegory. Iff Books.

Lönnroth Lars. Den Poetiska Eddan Gudadikter Och hjältedikter Efter Codex Regius Och Andra Handskrifter. Atlantis, 2017.

Ladinsky, D.J. (2002). Love poems from God: Twelve sacred voices from the East and West. Penguin Compass.

Mackenzie, Donald A. Teutonic Myth and Legend. Charles River Editors, 2018.

MacLeod, Mindy, and Bernhard Mees. Runic Amulets and Magic Objects. Boydell Press, 2014.

McFadden, Deanna, et al. Grimm's Fairy Tales. Sterling, 2011.

Meade, M., Meade, M. (2006). The water of life: Initiation and the tempering of the soul. Greenfire Press.

Metzner, Ralph, et al. The Well of Remembrance: Rediscovering the Earth Wisdom Myths of Northern Europe. Shambhala, 2001.

Monick, Eugene Arthur. Phallos: Sacred Image of the Masculine. Inner City Books, 1987.

Northern Star Constellations: "The Sky is not the Limit ..." Digitalis, www.digitaliseducation.com/index.

Ovide, and D.A. Raeburn. Metamorphoses: A New Verse Translation. Penguin Classics, 2014.

Prechtel Martín. (1998). Secrets of the talking jaguar: A Mayan Shaman's journey to the heart of the indigenous soul. Jeremy P. Tarcher.

Price, Neil S. The Viking Way: Magic and Mind in Late Iron Age Scandinavia. Oxbow Books, 2019.

Timothy Stephany's: Myths Mysteries Wonders, mythsmysteries wonders.site/ – Northern Star Constellations

Tolley, Clive. Shamanism in Norse Myth and Magic. Suomalainen Tiedeakatemia, Academia Scientiarum Fennica, 2009.

Shaw, M. (2014). Snowy Tower: Parzival and the wet, black branch of language. White Cloud Press.

Young-Eisendrath, Polly. Women and Desire: beyond Wanting to Be Wanted. Piatkus, 2001.

Wolkstein, D., Kramer, S.N. (1983). Inanna. Harper; Row, Publishers.